Space and Spirit in Modern Japan

Space and Spirit
in Modern Japan

Text and photographs by
Barrie B. Greenbie

Yale University Press
New Haven and London

Designed by Sally Harris
and set in Galliard type by The Composing Room of Michigan,
Grand Rapids, Mich.
Printed in the United States of America by Halliday Lithograph,
West Hanover, Mass.

Library of Congress Cataloging-in-Publication Data

Greenbie, Barrie B.
    Space and spirit in modern Japan / Barrie B. Greenbie.
    p.   cm.
    Bibliography: p.
    Includes index.
    ISBN 0–300–04122–5 (alk. paper)
    1. Landscape assessment—Japan.   2. Environmental psychol-
ogy.   3. Landscape architecture—Japan.   4. Human ecology—
Japan—Philosophy.   I. Title.
GF91.J3G74 1988
304.2—dc19   87–32041
                          CIP

The paper in this book meets the guidelines for permanence and
durability of the Committee on Production Guidelines for Book
Longevity of the Council on Library Resources.

10 9 8 7 6 5 4 3 2 1

Excerpts from *Requiem for Battleship Yamato,* by Mitsuru Yoshida,
translated by Richard H. Minear, reprinted by permission of the
University of Washington. Copyright 1985 by the University of
Washington. Excerpts from *In the Eyes of the East,* by Marjorie
Barstow Greenbie, reprinted by permission of the literary executrix
of the author, Alison W. Birch.

To Helen Partridge

One kind of definition of a good person, or a moral person, is that that person does not impose his or her fantasy on another. That is, he's willing to acknowledge the reality of other individuals, or even of the tree or the rock.
—Yi-Fu Tuan

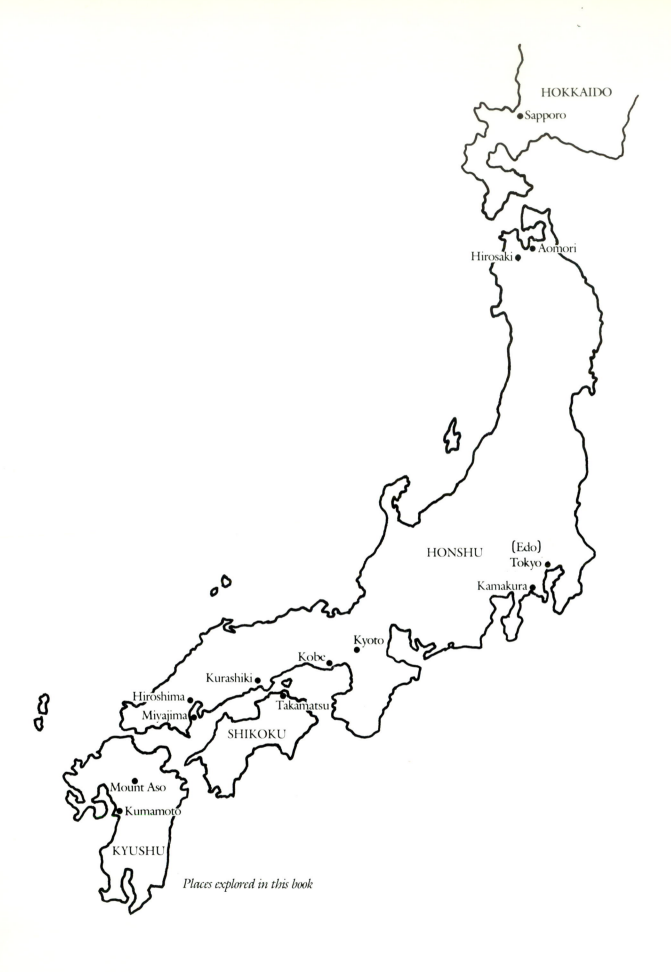

HOKKAIDO

● Sapporo

HONSHU

● Aomori

Hirosaki ●

(Edo)
Tokyo ●

Kamakura ●

Kyoto ●

Kobe ●

Kurashiki ●

Hiroshima ●

Miyajima ●

Takamatsu ●

SHIKOKU

Mount ● Aso

● Kumamoto

KYUSHU

Places explored in this book

Contents

Acknowledgments

As always in a work of this kind, many people have contributed in different ways. I can only acknowledge the most evident of these contributions.

I owe a very special debt to Yale University Press editor Judy Metro. Without her encouragement, support, and professional skill, this book would certainly not exist. She and manuscript editor Carl Rosen expertly disciplined my often too individualistic prose. Designer Sally Harris accepted, as she had on a previous book, my difficult request that photographs be laid out close to the text pertaining to them so that verbal and visual images make a common statement. For the second time, I feel fortunate to have a publisher for whom the production of a book is a collaborative, creative act.

Several people in America and Japan read all or part of the manuscript in various versions, providing valuable comments and suggestions. Jusuck Koh gave it a particularly thoughtful and helpful reading, which greatly stimulated and focused my own thoughts, as did Michiyo Matsuyama Connor. John Maki and Yukio Himiyama provided detailed factual observations on the entire text. Despite his disagreement with my premises and conclusions, Richard Minear generously gave a careful and very helpful reading of an early draft of the manuscript, and he also gave me permission to quote extensively from his translation of the Yoshida poem, *Requiem for Battleship Yamato*. Naoki Kurokawa not only commented on parts of an early version of this book, but also contributed an important bit of text along with photographs 50–53, the only ones that are not my own. Others who provided helpful and encouraging comments on early drafts of the manuscript are Shoichiro Asakawa, Nicholas Dines, Monica Jakuc, Mary Parker, Fumiako Takano, and Kayoko Yoshida. My thanks do not suggest that all of these readers necessarily agree with all of my observations; one clearly did not. The book is better for their help, but its faults of fact or logic are my own.

Four of the above were most helpful and hospitable guides during my visits to Japan. Yukio Himiyama welcomed me to the Hokkaido University of Education at Asahikawa and arranged valuable and gracious contacts in Kyoto, Nara, and Osaka by long-distance phone. He himself met me in, and escorted me around, Tokyo. I was shown other parts of Tokyo by Naoki Kurokawa, who specializes in traditional townscapes at Tokyo Metropolitan University. Shoichiro Asakawa organized and hosted a two-week stay in Sapporo when I was a guest of the University of Hokkaido. All three of these men and their wives entertained me and my wife most graciously in their homes. Fumiako Takano conducted me through various parts of Tokyo and the surrounding countryside and, with the staff of his landscape architecture firm, entertained me most royally in local establishments of that famous metropolis.

Eijiro Fujii showed me still other parts of Tokyo, and he and his wife entertained me hospitably at their home near Chiba University. Atsushi Ueda of Osaka University and Atsuko Tanaka arranged tours of Osaka, Nara, and Kyoto, and together they entertained me and my wife at Ueda's beautifully designed townhouse in Kyoto. Akinori Kato and Takashi Yasuda of Osaka University also conducted informative tours of Osaka and the surrounding region. Yasuo Masai showed me Tsukuba Science City. Koki Miida was most informative on city planning in Nara, as was Yuga Kariya in Kyoto.

During my stay in Sapporo I was entertained most graciously and informatively by Sadao Sakamura, Dean of Hokkaido University's Faculty of Agriculture, and by K. Tsutsui, Professor of Horticulture and Landscape Architecture at Hokkaido University, by alumni of their school, and by Takashi Sayama of the Hokkaido Broadcasting Company. Chiho Kaneko, a student of landscape architecture, was

a perceptive translator and a charming companion on these delightful occasions. I must thank Hokkaido University President Yoshio Ban and former President Mikio Arie for making all that possible. Mrs. Kayoko Yoshida of Arc Associates served as a most eloquent translator during a lecture I gave on the subject of this book at the university, and I am especially grateful to her for what I learned from discussions that followed. Mrs. Ayako Shimohirao of Sapporo's Park Department and Tadao Ariyama of Live Kankyo Keikau gave me an extensive tour of Sapporo's parks. Finally, on my route home from Hokkaido in the company of Shoichiro Asakawa, Ichiro Okuse of Hirosaki University in northern Honshu was an exceedingly generous host to the two of us for Hirosaki's famous festival. I am indebted to all these people for invaluable professional help and personal kindness.

I thank Takeo Tsuchiya of the Foreign Tourist Division, Japan Travel Bureau, for some perceptive insights into the life of Japan and the countryside surrounding the Inland Sea. I am also indebted to Otis Cary of Doshisha University in Kyoto for making interesting comments on Japanese life and the American influence on it and for arranging our stay at the Amherst House of that institution. I want to thank James White and Terumi Matsumoto for my restful stay at Tokyo's International House of Japan, where I did some of my research for this book. I also appreciate the assistance of Kenneth W. Duckett and Hilary Cumings of the Special Collections Department of the library at the University of Oregon in providing access to my parents' papers.

The front epigraph, by Yi-Fu Tuan, is from "Yi-Fu Tuan's Good Life," *On Wisconsin* 9, no. 1 (April 1987).

Most of all I want to thank my wife, Vlasta Koran Greenbie. She, too, was a valuable editor of the manuscript, she accompanied me on part of my travels and paid for some of them from her hard-earned savings, and she made other contributions too personal and numerous to list here.

1 • Introduction

The American scientist Edward S. Morse was one of the most sympathetic and perceptive Western observers to visit Japan in the late nineteenth century. He began his influential book on Japanese homes by declaring, "In the study of another people one should if possible look through colorless glasses; though if one is to err in this respect, it were better that his spectacles should be rose-colored than grimed with the smoke of prejudice."[1]

It is hard to see an interesting place through colorless glasses, especially a place with which the observer has had strong emotion-provoking associations. And it is especially hard to see Japan colorlessly, since artistry is that land's transcendent virtue, and art is always colorful, even when the color is gray. As all artists know, gray is produced by mixing opposite, complementary colors. Much of Japan is, in fact, a colorful gray. The unpainted woods of the traditional houses described by Morse, as well as the stones of the gardens that have so enraptured landscape architects, appear in bright shades of gray. Likewise, the Japanese culture itself is a mixture of vibrant, understated intensities.

In this book I will discuss Japan as I have seen it, not necessarily as it entirely is. I make no claim at all to being without prejudice. Prejudice can be for as well as against, and I will likely err on the side of the rose color. As a soldier in World War II, I once had ample opportunity to be aware of the dark side of Japanese culture, but my personal associations now are almost entirely with its bright side. I take it for granted that all cultures, like all individuals, have their dark side, and I hold with Morse that it is best as a general practice to look for the virtues in others and concentrate on the vices in ourselves. One learns more that way.

When I arrived in Japan for the first time, somewhat involuntarily in September 1945, I had already heard a great deal about it. My parents had both been journalists in Japan; indeed, it was there that they had met, so I can thank Japan for my existence. I grew up not only with stories and pictures of Japan, but also with a considerable written record of it. My mother's vision of the country was always romantic, but I can recall clearly my father's attitude changing from grudging admiration to prophetic anger with the Japanese invasion of Manchuria. I was seventeen when the news of the "Marco Polo Bridge incident" came over the radio and my father led me to a map on the kitchen wall, pointed to a spot in the South Pacific just north of Australia and said, "You will have to fight down there someday because of this!" Seven years later I found myself in Dutch New Guinea, just about where he had pointed, at a staging area preparing for the invasion of the Philippines. I landed at Subic Bay and fought as an artilleryman throughout the campaign to liberate Luzon and was scheduled to go on with the invasion of Japan, but I was spared that when the war ended with the atom bombs and the Japanese surrender. Instead, I was dispatched to Kyoto as a G.I. news reporter with General Kreuger's Sixth Army headquarters. By an improbable coincidence, I was billeted in a museum near the Heian Shrine, a few blocks from the Miyako Hotel where my mother had met my father one war earlier.

Writing of her experience there, my mother said, "It is well not to believe all one hears about Japan. It is still better not to believe all one sees."[2] On the basis of my own experience, I am ready to declare that it is probably all true, all one hears and all one sees and much that one does not, and that it is perhaps just as well to believe all of it if one is going to believe any of it. Japan, more than any other country I know, expresses in a carefully crafted way all the contradictions of human life.

Although the picture of Japan I will present in the following pages is shaped inevitably by my parents' view of it in their era and by my own recollections of it during the American occupation, it is primarily a view of late twentieth-century Japan. I offer it as a collection of personal observations on universal human responses to time and space as expressed in the unique Japanese culture. The objective is not so much to explain Japan as to discover how a close look at the landscape of that country can help us to improve our own world. I make no claim, however, to being an expert on things Japanese. Probably no one is an expert on Japan or any other country who has not lived much of his or her life in it. Possibly not even the Japanese fully understand Japan— but then, who among us can say with assurance that we understand ourselves?

For nearly a century and a half, the Japanese have been extraordinary among nations for a capacity to adopt both the cultural and technical ways of other peoples without giving up their own traditions in the process. This may be the real formula for their famed economic power, and it may also be the most significant rule of survival for any people in the modern world. On the whole, they seem to have learned far more from the West than the West has from them. In probing how the Japanese do this without surrendering their own ways of life, I offer the theory that led me to find certain principles behind the patterns I see in their landscape. We all have theories, whether we discuss them or not—even the Japanese, who seem less addicted to theory as such than are Westerners. However, the theory informing this book is intended to give structure to my observations rather than to explain empirical facts. I hope disagreement with all or part of the theory will not prevent the reader from taking the observations for whatever value they may have.

For two decades, the professional schools of universities concerned with environmental design—architecture, landscape architecture, city planning, and interior design—have attempted to cross the boundaries between art and science by introducing theories of human behavior and perception into the design curricula and thus into design practice. This has proved difficult, like the problems of communication that diplomats face in dealing with national cultures. Professions are subcultures, each with its own conceptual system and language. There is a large body of literature written by social scientists aimed at designers, but much of it is not intelligible, and even less of it is usable to working professionals.

In my book *Spaces: Dimensions of the Human Landscape*,[3] I tried to integrate the two different ways of looking at the world that C. P. Snow called the "Two Cultures."[4] I attempted to translate certain psychological and behavioral concepts, particularly those dealing with private and public boundaries, into design terms by relating them to actual places *visually*. The section of our brains that thinks in visual images appears to be partially separate from, and to follow a different kind of logic than, the part that thinks in words. In *Spaces,* I presented words and photographs in close complement so as to make the picture an integral part of the verbal statement, not a mere illustration of it, and the words something more than mere captions to the photographs.

In this way, I explored the relationship between small-scale social territories and the larger public landscape in my own Western world. My claims regarding this relationship, which will be elaborated on in chapter 3, have not to my knowledge been contested. But the question arises, does this relationship hold true for non-Western cultures? To answer this question, I returned to Japan in 1984 on a sabbatical visit to a very different country from the one I had left as a soldier nearly forty years earlier. During the long flight over, I tried with difficulty to focus my mind on the latter-day Japan of cars and computers among the shifting images of the battered Japan of my occupation stint, the enchanted Japan where my parents met, and the contradictory Japan my father talked and wrote about when I was growing up.

I thought of my father's angry warnings about the militarism that had emerged in the 1930s as I got my first view of Japan from the deck of a naval transport on 25 September 1945. We anchored in the cool, windswept harbor of Wakayama, ringed in by steep, rugged pine-clad shores and rocky islands, purple-brown in the haze, and I wrote home, "You can see where the Japanese artists—in the days when Japan produced art instead of armaments—got their inspiration."[5] The haze turned into rain and fog as we walked ashore, loaded with packs, rifles, and duffle bags, into a desolate landscape of bombed-out factories with not a soul in sight. Eventually we came to improvised houses amid blocks and blocks of rubble. The gray, silent people we met just looked at us dully. Despite the desolation, I noted that the rubble was neatly piled up, and the blasted lots were raked out. However, from unbombed Kyoto I wrote that we were "suddenly in a picture book world, not at all like the Japan we've been fighting." Although most people in Kyoto were hungry, poor, and depressed, the Japanese with whom we had direct dealings treated us more like honored guests than conquerors. Behind their courteous mask we could not tell what they were thinking, but we could guess. Most of us were more than willing to put the hideous war behind us, and the Japanese seemed even more anxious to do so than we were.

When, in 1984, my plane landed at the ultramodern Narita Airport, the contrast between what I saw and what I remembered was overwhelming. Nothing I had read had prepared me for the experience. A plushly upholstered bus took me to the brightly lit Tokyo Central Air Terminal, where a shiny taxi opened its rear door controlled from the driver's seat, its driver in a business suit, white shirt, and tie, white gloves holding a steering wheel under which a miniature red television was attached. The cab slipped smoothly into a stream of traffic, speeding past the glittering Ginza and into the Roppongi district (1), filled with embassies, to the International House. In that graceful institution, half hotel, half academy, a polite porter who would not take a tip opened the door to a small but elegantly simple room facing out on a genuine Japanese garden (2).

Not far from the International House is the Tokyo Tower (3). From the top, one looks out over the habitat of nearly thirty million human beings within a radius of thirty miles of the Emperor's Palace (4).

When I had last been in Japan, most of what can now be seen from that tower was rubble. More than half of Tokyo's housing stock had been destroyed. To the Western eye, the view of the present cityscape is one of stark contrasts amid miles of sprawl, but as with so much of the rest of Japan, there is more order than meets the Western eye. Acres of small tile-roof houses, with side yards as small as six inches, are packed like a crazy quilt among temples and cemeteries, warehouses and factories, huge screened tennis courts, and office skyscrapers towering over a generally low-rise urban landscape (5, 6). All this is laced with traffic-jammed arterials and superhighways and innumerable railroads that interconnect with remarkable efficiency and run constantly full of people.

1

2

3

4

My father in 1917 had complained of traveling about Tokyo in "dirty, crowded, creeping tramcars . . . so small that a passenger standing behind a motorman prevents him from using the antiquated handbrake."[6] Although he had admired the new central railroad station as being "modern in every way," on the streets he saw mostly legs in mud. With the utilitarian logic of the American, he lamented, "What an unsanitary state of affairs! With a moat and walls around an Imperial Palace large enough and extensive enough to have paved half the city, I saw not a paved street in the capital."[7] Today, one of the few extensive places in central Tokyo that is not paved is the area in and around the grounds of the Imperial Palace (7). Well before World War II, Tokyo had become a modern city, but in the aftermath of the war the "unsanitary state of affairs" caused by the bombing was extreme. The population of more than six million at the start of the war had been cut in half by the end of it, and when the evacuees returned, basic services were not there for

them. By 1962 Tokyo had become the first city in the world to top ten million people, and at that time one-fifth of the people still depended on wells, while nearly three-fourths had no sewerage.[8] That situation has been largely remedied.

The subways are clean and handsome, and they run rapidly, smoothly, and frequently. Connections are clearly marked to all parts of the city. At rush hours, a river of human beings fills the passageways like water through dam turbines, making rush hour in Manhattan seem lonely by comparison. The modern railroad station of my father's day now appears to be one of the more antique structures of the central area where it sits at the end of a wide boulevard facing the palace grounds. Temples and other prewar buildings that survived the saturation bombings (8) stand out in scale and texture from the general townscape, which is enlivened and colored by a dense tapestry of advertising signs (9). The streets are full of elegantly dressed people. Japanese fashion designers have taken over from

7

Paris and Milan. Women who shuffled about in kimonos and wooden clogs when I was last in Japan now swing down the street in Western-style trench coats.

But despite the dramatic changes, something indefinable had not changed, especially outside of Tokyo. Aboard the famous fast Shinkansen (bullet train) to Kyoto, I watched, floating by the picture

11

window, a mosaic of small houses, large factories, high-tension wires, small gardens, tent-covered fields of tea, dams, canals, highways, more houses, more factories, and rice paddies (10). Beyond lay the mountains. I saw the white cone of Mount Fuji, which my father had persuaded my mother to climb with him and on top of which he proposed to her. It was barely visible in the evening mists. The train pulled into a very modern Kyoto station, which I did not recognize at all. A taxi rolled down a broad avenue that I vaguely recognized, but that was now much more brightly lit. I saw the walls of the old Imperial Palace. The cab turned into a dark alley and stopped at the Amherst House of Doshisha University (11). After settling in my room, with its sliding *shoji* screens opening onto a Japanese garden, I walked out into the night. There, suddenly, was the Kyoto I remembered, a gray torii framing a narrow, dimly lit street with the dark wood houses, their delicate latticed sliding doors, the small planted yard spaces distinguishing public from private space under green or blue tiled eaves bordering canals (12, 13). Except for the immediate vicinity of the railroad station, Kyoto seems to me to have changed little in essence since my father's time.

What has changed and what has not changed in the Japanese landscape is a main concern of this book. For one to fully understand any representation of a landscape, whether it is described in words, photographs, or painting, one must have some awareness of the mind of the viewer. The "goodness" of not imposing one's own fantasy on others, noted by Yi-Fu Tuan at the beginning of this book, is no easier to maintain than other human virtues. It is not always easy to distinguish fantasy from reality, and, indeed, fantasy is merely one kind of reality. Science attempts to make the distinction between fantasy and reality as clear as possible, but that is also an imperfect process. The best the individual can do is to present his or her interior images as appropriate without insisting that they match those of others. In writing this book I have tried to integrate my personal reality with the kind of objective reality normally dealt with by science. My aim is to try to find in the richly segmented but strangely coherent landscape of Japan some general principles and patterns of human experience, expressed there in special ways, with which those of us who reside elsewhere might enrich our own environment.

One of the reasons it has proved so difficult for those charged with shaping the public landscape to utilize the findings of social science is that science and art deal with such different, often opposite, aspects of reality. Science is concerned with the general characteristics or properties of things. Design, especially the kinds of design we call *art,* is concerned with particular relationships between objects, events, and spaces. These differing aspects of reality seem to involve somewhat different modes of thought, for reasons that will be explored in more detail in chapter 3.

In comparing one culture with another, one comes up against a paradox. Comparisons can only be made on the basis of generalities; that is, by noting similarities and differences in the behavior and habitats of people taken as aggregations. But what makes cultures interesting are their unique qualities, which vary not only between cultures but also between individuals within those cultures. Not all Japanese (or Americans or Europeans), of course, fit the models that I have drawn up. Exceptions are important. Indeed, it is my premise that allowing adequately for exceptions to social norms is a basic task of environmental design. Generalizations are the basic stuff of science, without which we cannot make sense of the bewildering plethora of disparate impressions that bombard our senses even close to home, to say nothing of what happens when we travel abroad to a strange culture. Nevertheless, in our daily lives we move in a universe of particulars, constantly responding in a particular way. My central hypothesis is that the Japanese as a people understand these basic experiential contradictions and allow for them in both their behavior and the design of their living environments much more successfully than do "we in the West" taken as a collectivity.

A century and a half ago, before Commodore Perry opened up Japan to the Western world, the young French nobleman Alexis de Tocqueville visited the United States and wrote his astoundingly perceptive and prophetic *Democracy in America*.[9] Tocqueville looked at the America of the early nineteenth century to try to understand the changes that were then wracking older European cultures. He was favorably impressed by what he saw in America, but he saw social losses as well as gains, and he hoped that his book would help to minimize the losses without compromising the gains. He paid particular attention to a political generalization that had made the "new world" a symbol for the rest of the world: the ideal of *equality*. Tocqueville made a distinction, not then or now usually made, between equality and freedom. He noted that equality does not necessarily lead to freedom and that certain kinds of freedom are not only possible but facilitated in unequal societies. Tocqueville saw that majority rule does not necessarily lead to equality; the tyranny of the many could be just as despotic as the tyranny of the few, especially to those who happened to be numbered among the few.

The tyranny of the many in the mass marketplace is devastating for art in the modern world, particularly the environmental arts. Of course, public spaces in all cultures and at all times have been shaped by the tastes of those with the power to make decisions about them. The peculiar despotism of the mass consumer lies not in the fact that consumers share certain values—a desirable event in any society—but in the fact that these values are abstract generalizations which do not properly fit the particular lives of the majority that holds them. Such generalizations are summed up in the "real you" fabricated by the advertising industry. The problem lies not in the fact that commodities as such are mass-produced, but in that the taste for them is. This taste, manufactured on Madison Avenue far from homes and workplaces, usually does not reflect the various particularities of anyone's life. The majority absorbs this taste through the media and thus winds up tyrannizing over itself. Because this tyranny is exercised passively rather than actively, through indifference rather than censorship, it is all the more difficult to overcome. As Francine du Plessix Gray comments, "This marvelous country . . . leaves the artist utterly free to influence absolutely no one."[10] It would seem no coincidence that egalitarian social theories have emerged most influentially in nations whose economies are based on mass consumption, where diverse local economies are swamped by international economies of scale.[11]

Japan is now one of the world's leading constitutional democracies, but it is not an egalitarian society in the American sense. The Japanese view of the world—and human society within it—is essentially hierarchical. This hierarchical society, with its meticulous attention to status and deference to authority, has incorporated large industrial and high-tech systems into itself without being obliterated by them, thereby achieving some of the advantages of both. Hierarchy arranges parts so that each functions uniquely within an interacting, meaningful whole. In a collection of identical parts, no single part stands out because there is no frame or situation in which one functions separately from another in a larger order. Individual bricks in a brick wall, for example, remain unnoticed unless there is a varied pattern of bricks making up columns, cornices, arches, and so forth. To the extent that spirit is an expression of the unique configurations of parts in a larger order, spirit requires hierarchy to be manifest.

If an individual element or active agent is high in the scale of a hierarchy, it is concerned more with the whole than with the parts, yet it must respect and acknowledge the parts; without them there is no whole. It cannot require the subsidiary parts to be a duplicate of itself. So a kind of self-identity and dignity, or spirit if you like, must emerge in each element of the hierarchical system if it is to be efficient and well integrated. This is quite different from the Western idea of dignity based on the concept of a constant individual "self" that is manifest identically in any situation. A symbiotic relationship of parts to wholes and dominant to subordinate elements occurs in any coherently functioning system. Such a system can encompass actors or the settings in which actions take place.

The problem with societies that view *equality as sameness* is not that there are fewer talented people in the population or that talents are not developed in individuals who have them, but that the public does not look for talent in persons or in places. Not respecting individual talent, a society develops no collective talent. Basil Rathbone liked to quote the character he played so often in the movies, Sherlock Holmes: "Mediocrity knows nothing but itself. Talent instantly recognizes genius." Mediocrity is inevitable in a culture where the median is the ideal. The Japanese are obviously subject to all the pressures toward standardization that occur in an industrial society, and they have their own unique ways of being collectivized, but something in their culture resists being overwhelmed by standardization.

I do not, of course, recommend a return to feudalism. I myself am an American individualist, a product of my country's particular kind of open society, and I am well aware of its virtues and advantages. I have no illusion that I could live comfortably with the social and physical constraints the Japanese live with, however creatively. In this book I probe those aspects of Japanese life from which America in particular and the West in general can learn in the same creative way that Japan has learned from us, without surrendering what is vital in our own native cultures.

2 • Home Space

For all peoples, *home* is the center of domestic life, and the concept of home is generalized to the surrounding social territory in the idea of *homeland*. The evolutionary prototypes of these spaces in the animal kingdom are the nest site and what ethologists call the *home range,* the space shared by a pack, flock, or herd. For most of us, humans and animals alike, the home is the center of the homeland, and the homeland is the center of the perceived universe.

In the collective memory of each human culture as represented in its myths, time began when the homeland was created by whatever gods each culture claims as its own. Mythological Japan was first the home of the sun goddess, Amaterasu Omikami. According to legend, her direct descendant in a continuous line of symbolic rulers is the present emperor, whose main residence is in the Imperial Palace, Tokyo's central place. The palace is the symbolic apex of a spatial hierarchy in which the private home of each Japanese family is the basic module.

An examination of their houses can help us to understand how they manage relationships with each other and with the rest of the world. In their traditional houses, the Japanese have evolved a very special relationship between the home module and the surrounding public space, between "inside" and "outside." For many Westerners a house is a thing, an object, or as the Bauhaus theorists defined it, a "machine for living." But to the Japanese it is a context— or rather a shifting set of smaller contexts within a larger one. The traditional Japanese house changes with the hours and the seasons, like the light on the hills or the spaces under trees (14). In such houses, the landscape is not outside the house but part of it.

The traditional Japanese house is not a box with openings, as in the West, but a space-molding system. It usually has one, two, or at most three fixed walls, with one or more of the sides equipped with sliding panels that can be opened to the outside. The entire house resembles a Western porch that can be enclosed in winter by removable storm windows. In the Japanese house, this spatial transformation is accomplished not just seasonally, but at different hours for different circumstances. Inside, there are few fixed walls; interior spaces are likewise separated by sliding panels. Some of the exterior sliding panels are covered with translucent paper (now often plastic), which lets in a lovely soft light when closed. These are the well-known *shoji* screens, composed of horizontal rectangles framed by delicate wood sash. The house is made almost entirely of

14

wood, its post-and-beam construction clearly expressed as part of the design. For centuries the Japanese had used the "curtain wall" principle, now used in most steel-frame skyscrapers. This type of construction, where the frame carries the load instead of bearing walls, is also found in older American barns and many other vernacular structures around the world. But unlike in air-conditioned high-rise buildings, in the traditional Japanese house the system provides for flexible openings.

The floor platform, raised about eighteen inches above the ground on piers (15), is covered with straw *tatami* mats approximately three feet by six feet in size, roughly the area occupied by a reclining human body. The tatami mat is the basic building module; a room or entire house is measured by the number of mats it contains (16). The mats are straw in a soft textured beige, quiet to walk on, pleasant to touch and to sit upon, removable for cleaning.

When the sliding panels (*fusama*) that separate one room from another are moved back, two or more rooms become one large one. In the traditional house there are few rooms with fixed designations. Beds are simply mats and blankets spread out on the mat floor. Food is brought in on low tables or placed directly on the floor. Any room can become a bedroom or a dining room. There is a spatial hierarchy in which certain objects are placed in special places, as in the alcove called the *tokonoma,* and guests are seated according to rank, but this is more ceremonial than structural.

Because activity is concentrated at floor level, the shoji screens are usually translucent at a lower point than Western windows. When either the translucent or solid panels are moved back, the outdoors is clearly visible from floor to ceiling so that windows and doors are the same. Inside-outside relationships are thus integrated and highly variable, but edges and boundaries are also clearly delineated.

An important feature of the traditional Japanese house is the veranda, which according to Edward S. Morse is a word of Oriental origin.[1] The veranda, in Japanese *engawa*, is a narrow plank-covered platform, slightly lower than the matted interior floor but well above the ground. Above this, the characteristic projecting eaves protect the fragile shoji screens from rain (17), as do storm panels installed on the outside edge of the veranda and often closed at night for security. On upper stories a similar but slightly narrower platform serves as a balcony (18). At ground level, there is often a formal entry porch as well, but the verandas frequently have no railings, or railings over only part of their length, permitting one to enter or leave the building at many different points. When fully open, the structural house is a pavilion, a sheltered position in space rather than an enclosure, although it can achieve enclosure as desired in delightfully flexible ways (19).

17

The open walls typically look upon some sort of garden. Teiji Itoh, in *Space and Illusion*, writes in detail on the two different types of residential gardens: the "borrowed landscape" and the courtyard garden.[2] The borrowed landscape, in Japanese *shakkei*, means "captured alive," writes Itoh. The capturing of the qualities of things, inanimate as well as animate, and inserting them into a different context is the essence of Japanese art and design—expressing the spirit not only of trees and mountains, but also of wood and stone. The principle of the borrowed landscape is to frame some distant view with elements in the near and middle ground, making the faraway feature seem to be part of the surroundings of the house. Good photographers often do this either consciously or instinctively. A Japanese student once pointed out to me that I had created a borrowed landscape from a mountain two miles away from my home in Massachusetts by carefully pruning trees in the middle distance and organizing structures nearby (20). I had not thought of it that way. It is probably done naturally everywhere, but in Japan in the seventeenth century it became a formal principle of landscape art.

20

The other type of traditional home garden in Japan is the enclosed garden, which in some respects is similar to the atrium of ancient Rome and the courtyard gardens of Mediterranean countries. In Japan it has special qualities (21). It is separated from public space by structures, but it can be situated on one side of a building and enclosed on the other sides by a fence, rather than surrounded by the dwelling as in the typical atrium. The objective of the enclosed household gardens is to make the transition between public and private space less stressful and to allow the architectural interior spaces to blend in with the natural environment. These gardens are designed to make small spaces appear much larger than they are by the careful placement of details. Traditionally these include three elements: stepping stones, a stone lantern, and a stone water basin. Itoh notes that the common house garden in Japan evolved from the tea-house garden. In the sixteenth century the popularity of the tea ceremony became a way of spreading the culture of the aristocrats among the common people.[3] Unlike the Japanese "stroll gardens," designed to be seen sequentially as one walks through them (we will explore them in a later chapter), the courtyard garden was designed to be viewed from inside the house, as is the borrowed landscape, and thus to be a fixed extension of the home.

Initially, the tea garden was designed to be simple and restrained to avoid competition for attention with the tea ceremony itself. However, the entrance garden to the tea house is designed with sequential elements to enhance anticipation of the spatial (and spiritual) experience awaiting the visitor. The tea garden principle as applied to domestic architecture results in entrance spaces that are narrow and shaded, with an object like a lantern, basin, or distinctive plant only hinting at what is ahead, so that the openness of the house and interior garden comes as a delightful surprise (22). This progression from a narrow corridor to a space opening on an inward garden is well illustrated by an old house in Nara, which serves as the office of a city planner (23, 24).

Because the house walls are permeable and the surrounding space is visible from inside, domestic privacy requires that the garden be enclosed with a fence. The home space is thus defined by this garden fence, not the house walls. The garden space or its modern equivalent encompasses family life

22

23 24

and separates it from the public domain. Within the house is a special world that includes nature, nature beyond the platform floor and the sheltering roof, the nature of green plants, sky, wind, water, and stony earth combined with the manshaped forms of wood, paper, straw, and stone into an organic whole (25). But this whole is limited by the garden walls, representing the basic context of the family unit, the household, which in Japanese is called the *ie*, or family clan.

Within this unit of form-function the chief goal is harmony, consensus, belonging, or *wa*. The spirit of the whole defines the space in time, the *ma*. Everything outside of the garden walls is a different sphere. Even things that can be seen above the walls from within, the mountain of the borrowed landscape or the roof of an adjoining building, have a different character when they are viewed from outside the garden wall. Belonging to a different context they take on a different meaning.

Public-Private Boundaries

Of all the people on earth, probably none make as sharp a distinction between public and private space as the Japanese. The walls and fences that surround the house-with-garden, even under the most cramped conditions, delineate social as well as physical modules of their human landscapes (26, 27). These structures make up the texture of the townscape, even in crowded modern Tokyo (28). In the denser parts of small towns and big cities, some vegetation manages to work into the picture (29–30). The fenced-in household garden is as prevalent in the agricultural countryside as in the cities (31, 32).

The persistent Japanese custom of removing shoes before entering a house is a behavioral expression of these spatial public-private distinctions (33), separating the "dirty world" from the "clean world" and elevating the spirit as well as the body above the

26

27

28

29

30

31

32

ground. The floor of the house is not a floor in the Western sense, but a platform upon which one sits or walks (34). The view of the world from a sitting position at floor level is quite different from a chair-level position; for one thing, it is more humbling—one must be trustful of the surroundings and the people one shares them with to enjoy such a vulnerable position. Humility is restful too; at floor level one accepts the authority of gravity and the supremacy of the earth. The physical contact with the floor brings one into a sensual relationship with the structure of the house, just as picnicking on the grass brings one into sensual contact with the earth. The floor plane becomes a major part of the building design, visually and tactically prominent, rather than something out of sight "down there." Furthermore, sitting on the floor puts one in a different relation to spaces outside as well as inside the building. As noted, windows are virtually doors to the viewed world surrounding the house platform.

The Japanese architect Yoshinobu Ashihara attributes a special significance to the removal of shoes when entering a home. He claims it represents a central difference between Japan and the rest of the world that is manifest even in differing uses of building materials. He notes that in many parts of the world interior and exterior space have a certain homogeneity; in regions where attitudes and dress differ little depending on whether one is inside or outside, floors and walls are made of the same hard materials as streets, giving inside and outside much the same physical quality. It is a consequence of such homogeneity, he suggests, that shoes are worn both inside and outside, while to the Japanese the space where shoes are off is "inside," and the area where shoes are worn is "outside." Ashihara declares: "It is safe to say that most Japanese, when outside and wearing their shoes, feel an instinctive sense of formality, which they shed only when they take off their shoes upon returning to the familiar, relaxed world of the home. One might add that this custom derives from the spatial order of their houses—an order symbolized by the architecture of the floor."[4]

Ashihara maintains that the custom of removing shoes helps the Japanese retain this perception of spatial separation even when they live in Western-style modern dwellings. In Japanese apartments or townhouses, the entryway is lower than the main

33

34

floor, and shoes are left there while one puts on slippers and steps up into the interior. (This is also true in some public buildings such as restaurants.) Hungarian-born architect Botond Bognar observes that the visitor on the lower level is not regarded as inside the house even when the anteroom is behind the entrance door, and that "to invite one in, the host asks the guest to *agatte kudesai*, please step up, equivalent to the Western idea of stepping in."[5]

The removal of shoes holds a different and more fundamental symbolism in Japan than in most other places where it is practiced. Some other cultures also require or at least favor removing shoes, including at one time those in certain parts of central Europe. My Czechoslovakian-born wife has vainly tried to get me to remove my shoes when entering our house in semirural suburban America, but in the absence of widespread social pressure, I cannot keep this custom. To me it is a troublesome interruption of the continuity between inside and outside, which suggests that the perceptual distinction Ashihara draws is correct. However, my wife also says that in the time of her grandfather it was bad manners to take off shoes anywhere except in the bedroom. In the West it is generally considered bad manners to put shod feet on sofas, chairs or desks, which confirms that for the Westerner the floor is relatively insignificant.

There seems to be a paradox in that the Japanese achieve a fine integration between the inside and outside of buildings in the sense of relating structure to physical environment, but also make such a firm distinction between inside-as-private and outside-as-public in the social sphere. The paradox is resolved when it is considered that what Ashihara and other Japanese mean by "inside" also includes the garden and possibly a borrowed landscape as *seen* from the house. Everything perceived from within the surrounding garden fences is considered part of the home, and that can be privately inside even though it is outside the house platform and garden walls. What they consider "outside" is hidden by the fence, and the fence, not the building wall, defines the boundary between private and public. This sense of the domestic inner space hidden from the public way by fences is powerfully evoked in Lady Murasaki's classic *Tale of Genji*, written nearly a thousand years ago.[6] Within the house-with-garden home, the Japanese make a distinction between the elevated floor of the house and the surrounding earth. It is always the quality of the space, rather than the walls as objects, that defines "inside" and "outside." Of course, a house garden anywhere is likely to be more private than a street. But to my knowledge the boundaries are not so sharp, the meaning is not so important, and the distinctions are not so fine elsewhere as in Japan.

To the average Westerner, the house is an object defined by the building walls whether seen from within or without. Landscaping in the American suburbs generally consists of plants packed tightly against the foundations, rather than their use to define the spaces of "outdoor rooms." The English put great value on their home gardens, but these are spatially and perceptually distinct from the house, often barely visible from within it, despite the garden's importance for domestic welfare. Throughout the Western world, the townscape is primarily an aggregate of buildings-as-objects, although that was less true in medieval cities where buildings formed street spaces. Plants, where they exist, are not an organic part of the architectural space but serve as cosmetic embellishments to the house-object. In Japan, most of the planting is inside the fence, largely out of sight to the public, in the territory of the family.

Naoki Kurokawa, an architect who teaches at Tokyo Metropolitan University, has described to an American audience the carefully articulated transition zones between the public street and the house-yard as "gray space."[7] This space is especially important in homes, but it also applies to temples and more public buildings. By "gray," the Japanese mean intermediate between the opposites black and white (yin-yang), without the connotations of drabness so often associated with it. On the contrary, these all-important gray spaces, these transition zones and gateways, are highly textured, often intricately designed, and sometimes quite colorful (35). They often contain one or more carefully placed living plants. They have gates or arches, many with small roofs over them (36), and if, in the crowded streets, entrances are in the front wall of the house under projecting eaves, they often have hanging strips of cloth called *noren* (37), which let in air while closing the view.

35

36

37

38

39

All of this detail gives to the person entering a sense of penetrating an enclosure, of anticipation and surprise. The textures of wood and stone and plant, the curbs, stepping stones, and platforms, give kinesthetic intensity to the experience of crossing a threshold between environmental and social contexts. This happens not only in urban areas, but also in rural ones. It can be sensed in the traditional farmhouses, with their thick thatched roofs, smoke holes at the peak, and their serenely functional interiors that are clearly distinct from outside spaces, even when the outside is open country (38, 39).

It is the house as part of nature—a controlled, designed nature but no less natural for that—that makes possible the distinctions between inside and outside that Ashihara describes. The environmental wholeness of the traditional Japanese house makes the home a complete world unto itself, rather than a partial one.

Home Space, Family, and Society

Chie Nakane stresses that blood kinship is not the primary linkage in the Japanese family but is actually rather weak as a bonding force. (She contrasts this with China, where ties of blood are strong and extend over geographical space well beyond the house or the village or even the nation.) She says: "In my view, the most basic element of the *ie* institution is not that form whereby the eldest son and his wife live together with the old parents, nor an authority structure in which the household head holds power and so on. Rather the *ie* is a corporate residential group and, in the case of agriculture or other similar enterprises, *ie* is a managing body."[8]

A daughter-in-law, she notes, as a consequence of coming to live in the family, takes precedence over a natural daughter who has left to marry into another *ie* or to live somewhere else. Brothers can differ widely in social position and wealth because the obligation is to share within the environmental family unit, not in terms of blood kinship. Status depends first on one's social position within the group and second in the world at large. This is why, Nakane explains, family loyalties in Japan are readily transferred to the workplace, to the corporation. The workplace is a different frame from the homeplace,

obviously, but the essential function of the family group is maintained. Because of this, she asserts, the Japanese family system is not breaking down with modernization; rather it is simply transferring to new situations.

It might be worth noting that so-called blood ties are themselves conceptual abstractions. Genetic relationships, of course, are not determined by the bloodstream, but the point is that at one time in human history people were not even aware of "blood" relationships and did not know how babies were conceived, yet the family as a functioning system existed as the basic social unit. What really matters in human families are the personal associations established by living in them, recorded as emotion-laden memories in the limbic system. Even in ancestor worship, the Japanese usually honor recent ancestors whose actual lives impinged directly on their own, again stressing the personal, the particular connection, rather than the abstract one.

Security anywhere is paid for by restricted opportunity. Nakane and others note that the harmony of family life in Japan, in which all members including the authoritative head of the household must bow to the will of the group, does not mean that everyone is happy with the consensus. Personal frustration can run very high and can be all the more painful because it must be suppressed in the service of *wa*.

The film *Vengeance is Mine*, directed by Shakei Imamura, is an allegory of what happens to one who defies family authority and puts himself outside the group. In this film, set in World War II, local military authorities come to a fishing village to requisition boats. The young son of a Christian fisherman reacts with anger and defiance when his father, after an initial protest, gives up the family boat. The fact that the family is Christian, a small minority religion in Japan, is significant in this story, since all of its members are in a sense deviants. Perhaps the story would have been less plausible if the family had been portrayed as Shinto-Buddhist. After defying both his father and official authority, the boy becomes committed to an evil life. As he grows into a man he becomes a clever but unscrupulous impostor and a compulsive thief and murderer. Eventually he is caught by the law and, unrepentant, is executed for his savage crimes. At the end of the film, the father and the rebel's own wife, whom he had married against the family's wishes but who eventually had become the father's lover, ritually throw the dead criminal's bones off a mountainside. The bones hang in the air and will not fall. This man's soul cannot find a home in heaven, in hell, or on earth.

In any society the maintenance of a family identity requires some sort of space within which the family can exist as a unit, distinguished in its own eyes from other families. It has been long observed that delinquent street gangs in American cities develop a familylike social code based on peer values among youths who have no supervision from overworked or absent parents or other relatives. Their home is in effect the street. Although in Japan's crowded cities many of even the most traditional families cannot have the amount of space described above and live in compressed multifamily houses, until quite recently these were low, ground-hugging buildings, and a compressed form of garden space behind a private-public fence prevailed. It seems reasonable to conclude that the strength of traditional Japanese family ties is based on traditional home spaces and

that marked changes in those spatial relationships can have effects on Japanese society as profound as those in other countries.

Home Space in High-rise Buildings

There is no lack of prophets, both in and out of Japan, predicting trouble for the Japanese. Some doomsday pronouncements from outside its borders may be wishful thinking; success tends to breed both envy and fear in the less successful, even when it also brings admiration. Japan is alleged to be suffering from "advanced nation disease."[9] A Westerner married to a Japanese has entitled his book *Japan: The Coming Social Crisis*.[10] My own prognosis is that the greatest social danger facing Japan lies in the transformation of housing for their dense populations on a limited land area. As elsewhere, inert, shapeless, essentially spaceless high-rise apartment buildings are springing up in Japan's heavily urbanized areas. As in so many other countries, apartments are the only homes that many people today, even the relatively affluent, are able to obtain (40–42).

40

41

42

43

I was surprised to find that so many of these buildings lack the texture, proportion, and grace that is characteristic not only of traditional architecture but of most other modern Japanese design (43). Ominously, they lack the all-important spatial distinctions between inside and outside and public and private in a hierarchy of transition zones from house to garden to street characteristic of the older houses (44), including poorer ones (45), low-rise modern houses (46), houses in suburban areas (47), and even houses in crowded Tokyo (48). It is as if the Japanese have given in to the tremendous pressure

44

45   46

47

48

for housing and are providing mere storage compartments for human beings as so much of the rest of the world is doing. These apartments inevitably lack ground-level gardens or yards, and they also lack articulated transition zones between living units and hallways, the "gray spaces" described by Kurokawa, which are possible even up in the air. The hallways and entrance doors to the apartment units that I have seen are extraordinarily bleak compared with anything one finds on the ground, and even some of the very expensive units occupied by professional people are as starkly functional as our American low-income housing projects, although much tidier (49).

The biggest problem with high-rise buildings for residence is that they tend to prohibit any territorial connection between living units and the ground. These units lack transitional spaces between the home and the larger world.[11] I toured some tall apartment buildings in one Japanese city with Alice Coleman, a British geographer, in the company of a Japanese colleague, her former student Yukio Himiyama. Coleman had just published a book, *Utopia on Trial*, describing a monumental study of public housing projects in Britain, comparing them with traditional British urban housing. She and her associates had examined four thousand blocks of flats containing over a hundred thousand dwellings, which accommodated a quarter of a million people. These massive state-sponsored residential complexes have been

49

plagued with dreadful social problems in Britain as in America: crime, vandalism, litter, and uncared for and unsupervised children.[12]

Conventional social science wisdom is that such problems are the result of poverty, but Coleman's study, which expands earlier work done by Oscar Newman,[13] shows that building design exacerbates, if not causes, these problems. Prominent among the pernicious design factors are those pertaining to lack of family territory outside the dwelling walls. Her data strongly suggest that this element underlies all the other design faults she identified. As the three of us climbed the stairs and walked through the corridors of high-rise apartment buildings, Coleman kept checking off the design faults she had found in Britain. These particular Japanese buildings came out better than the English versions, but she noted a disturbing number of negative factors, all of them as contrary to the inside-outside relationships of traditional Japanese homes as their counterparts were to traditional British home design.

Japan, of course, has a criminal population, even a Japanese mafia, but it does not as yet appear to have the sorts of public street crime that have plagued American and many European cities. One of the things that strikes the foreign visitor is the general discipline of the population, especially the public honesty. Most observers attribute Japanese social discipline to the Japanese family structure. But, as noted, family structure requires a spatial framework in which all members of the family feel they have collective control, with children continually subject to the supervision of adults and presented with adult role models. Coleman, Newman, Jane Jacobs,[14] and others have shown this to be difficult to achieve in large, anonymous apartment complexes where children, once outside the house walls, are beyond the sight and the hearing of their parents, while often being within the sight and hearing of strangers who do not want them around.

In Hong Kong, where more than six million people are jammed onto an island of a few square miles, most people live in extremely tall buildings, and there the Chinese family system does seem to hold, making life workable if not contented. Japanese traditional culture has survived so many wrenching changes in the twentieth century that it may well survive this one too, and the evidence I have seen and heard suggests that it has so far. But many Japanese, as elsewhere in the modern world, are concerned with what they perceive as a breakdown of traditional values among the young, although to my knowledge they do not usually attribute this to residential design. I suggest that they should look into that connection.

Naoki Kurokawa informs me that typical government housing complexes are made up mainly of the working generation, those between thirty and forty years of age with children, and their environment provides little of interest for men in a society where public life is still largely male territory. Generational homogeneity has been typical of suburban life in America and elsewhere, and it has been deplored by sociologists. Kurokawa says that it runs counter to the Japanese social system. Nevertheless, he and his family moved from a single-family home to an apartment building in Yokohama to be relieved of the long hours of his commute to his job in Tokyo. Their new town, Tama Plaza, includes large tracts of single-family houses along with the public housing compound where they live and company flats built by corporations for their workers. Kurokawa says that his place has some advantages that may not be typical of others of its type, which were developed later by the Japanese Housing Corporation. The landscape has been well designed with some protection of the natural surroundings, and the residents are quite varied in their professions and activities. According to him, the traditional large family system is almost gone anyway. Old people still tend to rely upon their children financially and spiritually, but they are getting used to living by themselves after twenty-five years of high-rise life. In Tama Plaza, he says, "the intermingling of different classes, generations, and occupations is bringing us back to a more normal kind of community life."

Kurokawa's optimism for his neighborhood seems justified by what I saw of it. Although I found the architecture of the apartment buildings appallingly bleak in a very un-Japanese way, the general ambience of the community, with its leafy streets, especially around the commercial nodes, was quite cheerful and chic. Kurokawa's photographs (50–53) show the progression from the railroad station along some of the main streets to his building and the surrounding area. Photo 54 is my own picture of the Kurokawa family with my wife in their

N. Kurokawa

50

51

N. Kurokawa

N. Kurokawa

52

53

N. Kurokawa

54

apartment. The living-dining-family room suggests how cramped for space many people in Japan are by Western standards, despite high living standards in other respects.

I would have expected the balconies in this and other high-rise residential buildings to be used as substitute garden space, but as seen from the outside, plants on the balconies are remarkably few. When I asked another Japanese friend why there are so few plants in evidence on the balconies as compared with buildings at ground level, he replied, "Up there, there is no one to set boundaries against." This could be part of the answer, but if so, it is surely part of the problem. When windows face out only onto empty space, there is no hierarchy of zones in which the individual and the family are part of a social-spatial network, normally called a community.

Kurokawa reports that the Housing Corporation's standard for balcony width was set too low from the beginning, and that if it had been one and a half meters wide instead of no more than one meter wide, that affordable decision would have enabled people to use the balconies as semioutdoor spaces. Several recent studies, he says, have criticized this deficiency. However, Kurokawa suggests that the lack of visible greenery from the outside of these tall buildings is simply an indication of the continued emphasis on the inside world of the family. He wrote to me:

Almost all of the households maintain flowers and small trees in pots, spread all over the veranda floor. Many are very proud to show visitors their masterworks of Bonsai. We inherently prefer being surrounded ourselves by green ornaments rather than arranging them to face the people on the streets as German wives do in their town houses. Our history as an island people gives us an inherited sense of inward orientation, to stay within nature, within society, within the designed space, rather than attempting to control space by extending it outward in axes as the Italian and French baroque tends to do. Our world is composed of secluded units of space, each unit tied into a chain, and . . .

We see the invisible expanse of nature through the solid masonry walls. Don't make too much of this, but it is a wise and simple solution to the problems of living in a congested island country.

Actually, contemporary multifamily residences in Japan vary considerably in size, scale, and design.

55

56

57

One design conspicuous in Tokyo and other cities is a ziggurat style, which attempts to provide some outdoor family space (55). Others have tree-shaded yards, fenced play fields, and focused entrances at ground level (56), although they are a far cry from traditional design (57). Some have a hierarchy of

58

spaces of sorts and entrance courtyards off the city street (48). Still others stand by canals in the company of small homes in what may remain a coherent neighborhood (58). Ingenious ways of accommodating cars attest to the value of space as well as the value of private automobiles (59).

Like cars, single-family homes are greatly desired in modern Japan, as in American and European suburbs (60). A house with yard space, no matter how minimal, is the preferred form of residence for all classes. In northern Hokkaido, settled mostly in the twentieth century, the houses appear to be more free standing, like those in the American Midwest, but they nevertheless retain relatively secluded yards (61). Although it is hard to see its effect on the ground, the Japanese do have zoning; it is applied much more incrementally than is usual in America and Europe. New single-family homes continue to rise in small lots between big buildings, even in land-starved Tokyo (62). Green plants adorn even the most meager yard spaces around these. Their high-rise neighbors stand stark naked in their masonry skins (63).

59

60

61

62

63

The tremendous demand for housing of all types
puts dangerous pressure on good farmland. During
the American occupation, the large landholdings
were broken up, and farmers now work their own
earth. This had been done in theory during the Meiji
Restoration, but large tracts of land had remained
in a few hands. In the postwar period, a free
enterprise housing market coupled with tremendous
demand has led to farms giving way to residential
subdivisions at an alarming rate. Indeed, in urbanizing areas, heirs to farms are virtually forced
to part with some of the family acreage to pay high
inheritance taxes in urbanization promotion zones.

64

The value is on the land, not the house, and handsome traditional houses often go to the bulldozer to make way for apartments. But unlike America, large sections of agricultural land are rarely converted exclusively to residential subdivisions; the agriculture continues in the spaces between the houses (64). The farmer whose parents were peasants can become a millionaire just on the sale of his land alone.

Many modern Japanese have adopted Western furniture in their houses or apartments, which to

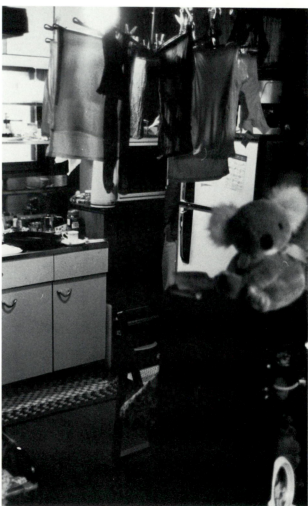

65

66

67

American eyes makes the small rooms appear crowded (65, 66). But children, at least, still sleep on the mat floor (67). Other families, perhaps most, prefer to sit on the floor in the traditional way in homes that retain some features of the traditional house, but with the appurtenances of a technologically advanced consumer society. A museum exhibit of finely crafted modern furniture suggests that floor-sitting is still very much in style (68). My wife and I found this to be the case in an elegant townhouse in Kyoto, designed by its architect-owner (69).

68

In the company of another Japanese friend, I visited a genuine Garden City near Tokyo built in the 1930s on Ebenezer Howard's English model. It had a nice Garden City feel, but with a quintessentially Japanese ambience, far more interesting architecturally than its prototypes in England (70). One house there had American-style picture windows facing the street. This is the only example of such an opening to the public way that I have ever seen in Japan, and even in this case the large windows were shuttered (71). In town planning as in other matters, the Japanese copy freely, but, with the apparent exception of the outsides of some high-rise housing complexes, most of what they copy turns into something uniquely Japanese. If Kurokawa's assessment of the emergence of a genuine community in Tama Plaza is at all

69

70

71

typical, Westerners who are also running out of urban space might do well to copy something from them in the same creative spirit, if we can apply their concepts to suit our culture.

Perhaps what is in the mind's eye matters most. Uniting the power of the conceptualizing outer brain with the inner emotional memory bank, the Japanese trap the traces of time within their living space by means of remembered tradition. To be able to see, as Kurokawa suggests, through solid concrete walls to the garden outside—that may be the modern Japanese secret.

3 • In the Eye of the Beholder

Traditional Japanese art and architecture, especially landscape architecture, are justly famous the world over. Japanese technical and economic achievements are equally famous, indeed probably more so, although they are frequently viewed with apprehension or hostility along with admiration. In a modern world where success in artistic matters is so often incompatible with success in practical or technical matters, how do the Japanese manage both? How are they able to participate in the increasingly abstract and impersonal relationships of international society without losing their native culture in the process? And what can the way they organize their own habitat tell us about this?

I can think of no other culture that manages to be so up-to-date and so traditional at the same time. I believe that has a lot to do with how the Japanese modulate the boundaries of their spaces, not only in their homes, as described, but also in their public spaces. They fuse the subjective landscape of feeling and sensation with the objective landscape of material fact in uniquely effective ways.

The hypothesis to be explored in this book is that the intimate Japanese house-with-garden, contextually separate from the more formal and impersonal environment of the public world outside it, actually reflects the neural geography of the human brain. Farfetched as it may seem to some, this spatial segregation of the subjective and emotion-laden activities of private life from the more objective, rationally ordered public ones may contribute to Japanese success in other respects. Territorial spacing of this sort may provide the mammal that resides in us all with the psychological security and personal identity of the nest site, without which the rational parts of our minds cannot function freely.

Underlying this hypothesis is the idea that all human beings actually live simultaneously and interactively on two levels of experience. One level involves direct physical contact with the environment, of both places and people, limited in scale to spaces and human associations in which one can interact sensually. On another level of experience, we respond to our environment and to other people in terms of abstract symbols, which are almost limitless in scale and are thus less governed by time and space.

For environmental designers, therefore, the human habitat in complex societies, especially industrial or postindustrial ones, can be divided conceptually into two qualitatively different but interactive kinds of spaces. One of these is the human expression of animal *territory,* which ethologists define as a *defended space*. Territories among animals can be defended by individuals or by social groups such as herds or packs, most commonly breeding units. In human societies, social territories are often called "neighborhoods," "communities," or "villages," which in heavily populated areas appear as subunits of cities or regions. However, there are, and probably always have been, large portions of the human landscape that are not primarily defended spaces, particularly along travel corridors that connect local communities and often penetrate them while being functionally outside their boundaries. It is on this geographical level that human behavior differs significantly from that of other creatures. The Japanese, as I perceive them, organize their living landscapes more effectively than many other peoples, allowing for these qualitatively different kinds of social space.

A few years before humans first stepped on the moon, thereby extending mankind's nonterritorial space beyond the earth's atmosphere, a small group of popular writers began to publicize the discoveries of the relatively new science of ethology, the study of animal behavior in the natural habitat. In 1966, Robert Ardrey's *Territorial Imperative* created a flurry of controversy in the social sciences.[1] It raised the bugaboo of human "instinct," heating up the so-called nature-nurture debate that has flared off and on ever since John Locke's tabula rasa was written upon by Charles Darwin (pun intended). It occurred to me that if there was such a thing as a "territorial imperative," those of us who spend our professional lives as planners putting boundaries around human activities, and as architects enclosing them with walls, might do well to learn as much as possible about it. In 1970, I traveled about to this end, talking to natural scientists.[2] The more I learned from these scientists, the more it seemed to me that humans do behave remarkably like other animals, but it also became increasingly clear that we behave in ways that are remarkably different. It was not until I came upon the work of the neurophysiologist Paul D. MacLean, director of the Laboratory of Brain Evolution and Behavior for the U.S. National Institute of Health, that this paradox began to resolve itself. And it is a true paradox, one that appears to be wired by evolution directly into the human brain.

The outer human brain, the cerebral cortex, is divided into two hemispheres performing somewhat different cognitive functions. Artists in particular are familiar with the theory that one side is dominant, controlling speech, mathematics, and logical thought in most people, while the nondominant side (usually the right hemisphere in right-handed people) directs spatial behavior and artistic pursuits.[3] This has been hailed in the popular press as a great new discovery, especially since R. W. Sperry received a Nobel Prize with two others for his contribution to it in 1981. But I can testify that the basic concept is at least fifty years old; in 1934 I was the patient, pupil, or "guinea pig" of Samuel T. Orton, who I believe was the first scientist to observe and investigate the phenomenon.[4] Orton was extremely kind and helpful to me as a left-handed schoolboy with dyslexia having trouble with the three Rs. But in 1934 his theories were viewed as witchcraft by the Guardians of Truth in my school, and I did not have the kind of help now available to dyslexic children. (However, Orton got me off the hook for poor grades in the minds of my credulous parents.) The experience has left me with a lifelong interest in the human brain.

Although I am an amateur on this profoundly intricate subject, it appears to me that MacLean's theory of the *triune brain* greatly expands and deepens the concept of cerebral bilateral dominance, which is now scientifically respectable. MacLean has found that the distinctively human "thinking cap," the highly evolved but bifurcated outer cortex of the brain—which allows us to think with one hand without always letting it know what the other hand is feeling—surrounds and encloses older neural centers that are remarkably similar in chemistry and structure to those of lower animals. Of particular significance is the inner area known as the *limbic system*, common to all mammals, which appears to be the basic seat of emotions. MacLean believes that in normal people these neural regions interconnect and transmit information to each other, but to some extent they function independently.[5]

Emotion in mammals apparently evolved to bond parents and young with ties of affection in order to assure the survival of offspring, which need more care than the young of egg-laying species. Also, emotion seems to enlarge the memory bank by enabling mammals to attach feelings to events and places in more complex ways than is possible for lower animals. The limbic system seems to be a "time machine" for mammals. A momentary sight, sound, or smell can often induce in humans the recall of scenes that were once associated with strong emotions. We can sense that a similar phenomenon occurs in the mind of the family dog. But, as far as we know, the brightest dog cannot draw abstract conclusions from such recalled experience, certainly not to the extent that the least-endowed sane human can. In MacLean's view, this is because abstract thought is processed primarily in the outer layer of the brain that is highly developed only in man.

MacLean notes, for example, that people suffering epileptic seizures of the interior limbic system can perform complex intellectual functions and yet remember nothing of having done so. Presumably in this and other kinds of amnesia, the outer cortex keeps functioning while the emotional inner brain malfunctions, and memories attached to emotions are blocked or obliterated. By contrast, people whose rational outer brains have been damaged by disease or accident, such as a stroke, can live full emotional lives, often painfully so. Early on in my own investigations, I asked MacLean how his theory of a brain composed of imperfectly integrated layers, like those of an onion, relates to an outer cortex divided into functionally separate halves. He responded that the "artistic" nondominant side of the outer brain maintains closer contact with the internal emotional limbic system, being led around by the dominant side, in his words, "rather like a lazy tourist." It appears that the dominant half of the outer cortex deals with the three Rs because that is the half that pays attention in school, while the nondominant half, remaining plugged into the emotional world of the inner brain, looks out the window and daydreams about a landscape of spaces filled with feelings and images. Artists, it seems, more nearly utilize both sides of their outer brain and thereby integrate the sensual, kinesthetic mode of experiencing the environment that is tapped by the nondominant side with the abstract symbolic forms of thought that are expressed verbally or mathematically.

The Japanese physician Tadanobu Tsunoda, a specialist in audiology and the relation of hearing to language, has carried on the work of Sperry and others by means of his novel experimental method that uses sophisticated audiological technology. In *The Japanese Brain*, Tsunoda presents the theory that the Japanese, because of unique characteristics in their language having to do with a heavy emphasis on vowel sounds, typically process human emotion-evoking sounds and sounds existing in nature along with verbal sounds in their dominant left hemisphere, whereas Westerners relegate these to their nondominant right hemisphere.[6] Tsunoda makes no claim that the Japanese brain is genetically different from anyone else's—indeed, he clearly states the opposite—but only that it develops differently in the first eight years of life under the influence of language. (He includes Polynesians as developing similarly.) His observations seem to conform well to widely accepted theories of developmental psychology, and I believe anthropologists agree that language profoundly affects human cultural behavior. Tsunoda nowhere claims that this peculiarity of the Japanese and Polynesians makes them superior, and he strongly appeals for respect for human cultural differences. Indeed, I wish he had done more to suggest what his conclusions lead to.

Tsunoda's findings could explain the artistic achievements of Japanese culture through the centuries. Art can be defined as a fusion of emotional feeling with certain kinds of logical thinking. If this occurs on the dominant side of the brain instead of being split over two halves with one half subordinate, it is reasonable to conclude that artistic expression will be facilitated. In my view, art is the preeminent way in which all human cultures bridge the gaps that may exist between the thinking and the feeling brains.

MacLean's work goes much further for my purposes than the discoveries of Orton, Sperry, and Tsunoda. MacLean's work is controversial for at least one brain researcher, mainly on the niceties of neural circuitry that no layperson can comment on with authority.[7] That emotional responses originate in the limbic system is widely accepted. No doubt scientists in this field agree that the human brain is the most complex entity in the known universe and that science has not even begun to explain all of its mysteries. I present MacLean's theory not to advocate it, which I am not qualified to do scientifically, but because it is through this theory that I arrived at the spatial concepts I develop in this book. My central theme pertains to readily observable ways in which human beings organize their habitats, not to brain structure as such or any particular psychological theories. Almost anyone will agree that one often thinks logically in ways that run counter to emotional feelings. Whatever the final explanation may be, the phenomenon itself is hardly arguable. It seems to me that MacLean may have found a physiological explanation for otherwise unexplainable experiences we all have and for such arcane concepts as Freud's id, ego, and superego and Jung's archetypes. However, my reason for presenting MacLean's theory in connection with this and earlier discussions of space is that it has enabled me to see relationships that I could not have understood without it. Nonetheless, all the ideas offered here, including and especially my own, are given only as hypotheses, not revealed truth. I do not view any relationship between physiology and culture as wholly deterministic. It is amazing that so many similar inner structures can give rise to such a diversity of outer forms. However, one's comprehension of form is enriched by an awareness of underlying structure, like the skeleton under the flesh or the flesh beneath the clothes.

References to social biology are likely to be looked on with suspicion because genetic theories have often been invoked to justify arguments for racial superiority. I myself have never seen a shred of evidence to suggest that any race is inherently superior. It seems to me that racial differences are miniscule compared to similarities; we are, after all, one species: Homo sapiens. Recently, this touchy matter has been aggravated by the comments of Japan's prime minister Nakasone regarding racial diversity in America, which caused a storm of protest here (and a considerable amount in Japan), all at a time of growing tension over trade policies. Although in this book I present Japanese culture in a favorable light, I most certainly do not attribute its virtues to any genetically derived superiority in Japanese brain structure. My argument is exactly the opposite: Japanese culture has evolved uniquely effective ways of expressing the workings of the *universal human brain*.

The main premise of this book is that on the emotional and sensual level of experience, man seeks and requires spatial limits, boundaries, while abstract thought is indifferent to boundaries because it cannot be contained by them. Thus, designs for the kind of spaces that satisfy sensual needs (presumably mediated primarily by the inner, older brain) require close attention to edges and enclosures and idiosyncratic local symbols, whereas designs for the kind of spaces perceived in terms of abstract concepts (presumably mediated by the outer cortex of the brain) should focus on openness and accessibility, since the forms of such spaces are most likely to elicit universal human understanding on the purely rational level. I think that has been the case with the appropriately named International School of architecture. However, the appeal of such spaces will always be limited because they do not usually satisfy emotional needs. The significant thing is that at best the two kinds of space are interactive, dialectically interpenetrating and mutually reinforcing poles of a continuum, not mutually exclusive opposites. They can occupy the same geographical area, and one can turn into the other depending on the situation. In my view, highly rationalized cultures that deny the elementary need for bounded territories drive that need underground, where it becomes dangerous for the public welfare. The failure to recognize social territories, then, actually works against the formation of civilized cosmopolitan spaces.

In the age of Einstein, we cannot consider space without considering time. Heisenberg noted that a thing changes in the process of observation, at the moment of awareness, and so nothing can be known exactly. But the mind retains a record of previous moments and past realities, linking them with eternally new realities in the present. Part of this record is maintained by the structures and other objects that humans place in their environment.[8] The mind thus introduces the dimension of time into space. Paradoxically, Japanese culture, which puts so much emphasis on the emphemeral (symbolized by the briefly blooming cherry tree) and consequently on life in the moment, is peculiarly aware of time. Their central environmental concept, *ma*, involves not simply the harmony, *wa*, of objects in space but also the harmony of objects in time.

Indeed, my Japanese friends maintain that time and space are not separate but a single entity, time-space, or *ma*.

All animals, because they move, must deal with space. They also have internal biological clocks (as do plants) that govern their responses to the environment at various times. Higher animals, especially mammals, have memories that encode experience over time, and their bodies, moods, and behaviors change with circadian rhythms and with the seasons. But their awareness of the past must be limited compared to man's because they do not have language with which to record memories (the basis of literature); they have little or no way of maintaining physical records (as in architecture or artifacts) except through changes in their bodies; and their brains have not evolved to deal significantly with abstractions, with concepts as opposed to sensations. It should be noted that the degree to which animals other than man conceptualize is currently a subject of debate among ethologists.[9] Various studies, particularly those of Jane Goodall on wild chimpanzees, have revised old assumptions about the uniqueness of human beings in this regard.[10]

In his fascinating, important book, *The Dance of Life*, Edward T. Hall describes several different ways in which various human cultures experience time.[11] Hall notes that differences in perception and behavior result from contrasting time systems and can lead to conflict between members of different cultures, especially between Western societies, which Hall calls AE (American and European), and other societies that are often called "traditional." But Hall infers that there is also an underlying common human experience of time. My own interpretation is that this common experience is closest to the biological rhythms mediated by man's "animal" inner brain, while cultural differences are generally the consequence of the ability to conceptualize abstractly, although some cultures are more responsive to emotional and biological rhythms than others. Thus, in my view, it is in biology, not culture, that our common humanity is most pervasive, and I discuss the implications of this below. For the present purpose, I think it is safe to say that the concept of *time* in all its cultural manifestations is an invention of the human mind to account for something that only the human brain itself can comprehend, because, as I have noted, only humans can maintain a (relatively) permanent physical record of life experience in space. Indeed, one definition of architecture and landscape architecture might be the art of recording human experience in time-space.

The increasingly impersonal relationships on which modern industrial and commercial societies depend are based largely on abstract concepts not only of time but also of objects and activities and the spaces in which they occur. Perhaps the most ubiquitous and influential of these abstractions is money. A dollar or a yen does not describe or physically correspond to a car, a camera, a computer, a meal in a restaurant or the restaurant building itself, or the land on which the restaurant sits, yet it can be used to measure the relative value of these things. Money can measure labor in units of time (hourly wages), which can be exchanged for material things and human services. Furthermore, dollars, yen, and other currencies can be interchanged more readily than the goods and services they represent. Mathematical or technical symbols can be used in a similarly abstract way in a wide variety of situations; they can be used by different peoples on a worldwide scale precisely because they are generalizations largely independent of the particularities of time, place, and culture. Thus, on the conceptualizing level, there is a common dimension to human affairs that transcends tribal culture. However, what leads us to design anything in a particular form and to prefer one form or another is not abstract or generalizable. Our strongest motivations are derived from the sensual experience of the particularities of our individual lives in close physical engagement with our tribal territories and the people we share them with.

In terms of time and space, one significant aspect of MacLean's theory is that the rational outer cortex of the human brain processes information at a much faster rate than the older inner brain centers.[12] It seems that the outer human cortex is a superior computer in the quantity of information it can handle in a given period of time, although the quality of the information is not necessarily superior. Because the outer brain can apparently process information faster, it can cope with space on a larger scale. Consider, for example, the amount of information needed to navigate an ocean by sailing ship compared with swimming across a lake. The information it takes to go to the moon already exceeds the capacity of any human brain and cannot be handled without computers. By contrast, the kind of information that most affects feelings and the intuitive type of understanding derived from felt experience is obtained by direct physical contact with the environment and therefore needs time to be absorbed into the memory bank. It also requires spatial limits in that the process of storing experience in memory is facilitated by repeated contact with the same environment.

Hall has observed that some unconscious biological responses are actually faster than conscious logical responses.[13] However, the perception of time relevant to this discussion does not involve the culturally specific moment-by-moment communication Hall considers so much as the length of time it takes to aquire the attitudes, perceptions, and life experiences on which that type of communication is based. In particular, it takes time to genuinely love anyone or anything, including a place, time to build up the necessary emotional associations. The older inner brain must acquire knowledge concretely, through all the senses, including and especially the senses of touch, sound, and smell. A trained human mind, however, can take in the abstract characteristics of unfamiliar objects and events and make associations at incredible speed once a conceptual system has been established. This is normally achieved by visual signals and often at a distance, precluding close inspection through the other senses. Presumably the outer portions of the human brain generalize from shared characteristics, disregarding particularities to form the abstractions. The problem is that the abstractions can replace other kinds of symbols in the culture. The price of abstraction is that in the process of creating it we often eliminate from the subject under consideration much of the feeling that makes familiar things, places, and events dear to our hearts.

It seems that the Japanese do not abstract at the expense of feeling, at least not to the extent that modern Westerners do. The Japanese appear to acknowledge in their own behavior and in the arrangement of their habitat the contradictions inherent in MacLean's brain, whereas Westerners tend to deny those contradictions. Paradoxically, by accepting the contradictions, on some levels the Japanese achieve a unity of experience that eludes us. Tsunoda's findings suggest to me that by responding to environmental stimuli along with logical thought, all in the left brain, the Japanese unify rather than compartmentalize experience. But my argument is precisely that imaginative unification, or synthesis, requires the perception of differences and, at the same time, a holistic handling of those differences.

Western culture since the Enlightenment has tended to elevate the social status of rational thought and to make emotions suspect. Indeed, the idea that we have an animal brain is repugnant to many people, and that aversion probably underlies the quite emotional controversies generated in some quarters by social biology. It is less likely to be an offensive idea to those Japanese Shintoists who traditionally have found kindred spirits, *kami*, not only in all living things but also in inorganic objects. In the West, to be reasonable and objective is usually considered nobler and more moral than to be emotional and subjective. The Japanese do not appear to make these judgments. Because they are able to segregate conflicting behavior patterns spatially, it may be easier for them to act rational and detached in one set of circumstances and sensual and emotional in another. Many other cultures, especially the so-called primitive ones, elevate emotional and sensual experience as the prime reality, but they do poorly at the kinds of objective technical activities that depend on rational judgment. The Japanese apparently maintain a balance, although, as with all they do, it is an open-ended asymmetrical balance. To the Japanese everything is *contextual*.

The ability to think abstractly, to generalize from one set of experiences to another, is a marvelous characteristic of the human imagination, the one that beyond all others sets us apart from other living creatures. In industrial and postindustrial societies, people share elaborate symbolic systems that transcend local and national boundaries and social conventions. This is possible, as I have noted, because they are abstractions to some extent detached from local specifics. The problem is that because the symbolic systems of international trade and technology can be so devoid of sensual reality, the

products and especially the environments that result from them tend to be emotionally empty, even when they satisfy certain physical and even psychological needs more effectively than traditional local economies. The satisfaction of basic desires in such a dull way leads to a peculiar restless malaise that is widespread in advanced nations, while the normal human need for sensual stimulation and experiential variety is met with gaudy mass-produced trivia. The environmental psychologists Stephen and Rachel Kaplan sum up the situation: "Indeed, it might be argued that in the modern world, the interesting is no longer important, and the important, no longer interesting."[14]

Japan suffers intensely from all the objective evils of industrialization: environmental pollution, unbelievable congestion, noise. But although it has become a master of mass production, most of its urban environment manages to remain interesting in a way that the contemporary environments of the West or of Eastern places such as Singapore do not. No matter how disciplined the Japanese are in systematizing technology, they do not let it overwhelm the sensual, emotion-provoking aspects of experience and the sense of historical time.

Although the Japanese have developed immensely efficient manufacturing systems, currently beating the West at its own game, their products are the least standardized in appearance of those on the international market. They have introduced into mass production some of the variations of detail that characterize their traditional art and architecture, retaining in large production systems that sensuous particularity which all along has been the most distinguishing feature of things Japanese.

For example, the traditional stepping stones of a pond in a sacred garden force one to watch one's feet and, as a consequence, to look down and see the water. An abrupt change of direction at midcrossing leads one to see first one view, then another. Similarly, a Japanese meal is not a stew, but a series of separate foods—fish, vegetable, noodles, rice, meat prepared in its own sauce—each cooked to bring out the flavor of that particular food in a way that stimulates all the senses: sight, smell, touch, sound (as in the pouring of tea), and taste. As the world's second-largest producer of automobiles, the Japanese are first in the variety of models, shapes, sizes, and driving characteristics produced, in diversity far ahead of the technically advanced Americans, Germans, and Scandinavians. In the sensuality of their car designs they are well ahead of the French and Italians. This most likely has as much to do with their marketing success as with their pricing and other trade practices. But their cars are also mechanically efficient and dependable, unlike some handsome British and Italian sports cars. The Japanese standardize what matters most, without standardizing what cries out for diversity, in their industrial products as in their lives. I think that this is because they keep the experiential domains I have discussed partially separate in space. By keeping them separate, they are able to unite them in specific contexts when that is appropriate and desirable.

This separation is puzzling and disturbing to many Westerners, whose traditional thought processes are dedicated to the pursuit of transcendent universals, a single God in religion, a unifying theory in science, and a universally applicable formula for dealing with economic, social, or environmental uncertainties. Japanese traditional religions are a complex tapestry of myths blending Buddhism and Confucianism with a pantheon of animistic gods. Some Japanese have no trouble being Buddhists, pagans, agnostics, and Christians simultaneously, invoking ideas to suit the situation.

Japanese social anthropologist Chie Nakane has specialized in studying her own culture. She notes that Western observers of Japan tend to separate Japanese society into conflicting traditional and modern outlooks with the general assumption that when Japan becomes fully modern it will be just like the West. She maintains that Japan remains a well-integrated entity in which the traditional and the modern are simply separate aspects of one reality.[15]

Nakane uses the English terms *attribute* and *frame*. Frame, she says, is an imperfect translation of the Japanese word *ba*, which means *location* but also *situation* in the sense of its having a particular purpose or function. The term *attribute* as she uses it refers to the individual's characteristics carried into the frame or situation. In a rural setting, the village itself is the frame, and the individual's family group or caste is the attribute. In an urban corporation, the company is the frame, and the individual's position in the company as executive, engineer, or machine operator is the attribute. In Japan the frame takes social precedence over the attribute; a Japanese person identifies himself or herself first as belonging to the company, and only then as an executive or engineer. Nakane observes the opposite in India; there, the attribute takes precedence. In America, with the mythic emphasis on individualism, attributes come first, although not those that depend on inherited social rank. I believe that Americans, in stressing attributes so strongly, tend to make inadequate distinctions between one situation and another.

I prefer the word *context*, a favorite term of landscape architects and many building architects, and I use it in the sense of Nakane's *frame*. The Japanese emphasis on the primacy of frame, situation, or context, as I see it, enables them to work with the inherent schisms of the human brain. They achieve an overall unity of experience, not by insisting that individual attributes fit all circumstances consistently, as Westerners tend to do, but by moving adroitly from one situation to another, altering their behavior—in other words, their attributes—accordingly.

The paradox is that in so doing, the Japanese retain a consistent inner quality, which for lack of a concrete term can be called *spirit*. Americans are trapped by the contradictions of life because we do not admit and accept them. We often lose, or fail to recognize, the spirit of things in a continually changing world because we think we must always wear one face. That face is an abstraction, the one the advertising industry mass-produces as the "real you." I suppose that most of us in Western cultures are aware that we act and feel like quite different people in different kinds of company, and that although there is a consistent core of personality within us, only a portion of that is revealed at any one time. But we allow our social conventions to convince us that what is in actuality a mask is the true reality. That leaves us nothing under the mask. The Japanese deliberately put on a range of masks, not to conceal the inner reality but to express it appropriately in a particular situation. In all societies, presumably, the best of manners perform that function, but the Japanese do it in a more carefully contrived way than any other people I am familiar with. Those who know the Japanese often observe that what some Westerners perceive as coldness or impassiveness actually protects intense, sensitive feelings. The Japanese are using abstractions rather than being used by them.

The emotional centers of the brains of mammals have been designed by nature precisely to make these animals flexible in coping with the changing realities of the environment. By coding events in time and space with feelings, the enlarged memory bank enables mammals to respond adaptively to the particularities of experience rather than reflexively in a genetically programmed way, as simpler creatures must. In man, the still more advanced human cortex has evolved to deal with generalizations from experience, with the common characteristics of things rather than with their uniquenesses. These generalizations have been immensely useful to our species, but now, in all developed countries including Japan, there is a growing backlash against the consequences. The reaction of some Japanese to mass-consumer standardization was forcefully expressed by Eiko Ishioka and Arata Isozaki in the traveling exhibit *Tokyo: Form and Spirit*, in which a collage of working television screens flash duplicate images of commercials under the glass floor of a representation of a Noh stage, while a large television with the same images occupies the place of the god in a futuristic rendering of the sacred space of a Shinto shrine.[16]

Throughout the industrialized and commercialized world, emotional rejection of the technocratic and bureaucratic abstractions of modern life is increasing. Public social agencies in the United States, in their efforts to serve large anonymous populations, use the term "delivery systems." One can visualize a tractor-trailer truck, backed up to a loading dock, distributing boxes of social service goods to replace the personal contacts of priests, physicians, and leaders of traditional communities. In regard to the environment, there has emerged a worldwide preoccupation with what is imprecisely called "human scale." This scale pertains to relatively small, intimate spaces, enclosed by sensually textured surfaces, which are conducive to personal social relationships. But in terms of MacLean's brain theory, we should look upon this as *mammalian* scale because it is the scale on which we can interact with

others and our surroundings in terms of feelings aroused by sensations, as do other mammals. We must maintain this scale because we will continually feel unsatisfied without it. But we must also maintain the larger conceptual scale to survive in the world we have constructed with our abstract systems. It is not an either-or situation: both are necessary, and to maintain them we must recognize that they are different.

The truly human scale is that of the magnificent vistas of possibility that occur when emotions are joined to abstract thought. This juncture occurs, I believe, when we create real art, and it is also manifest in the most creative science. The Japanese have an unusual capacity to achieve this fusion. Traditional Japanese environments are particularly rich in the mammalian scale. This is true of most preindustrial cultures, but the Japanese are unique in the extent to which they retain this scale with modern design technologies. My hypothesis is that their ability to compartmentalize experience in space enables them to solve abstract technical problems in abstract technical ways, while holding to their deep-seated cultural traditions on the domestic level.

Much has been made of the "groupiness" of the Japanese. The family unit has been important historically to Japanese society, as it has to most cultures, although it is alleged to be disintegrating in Japan's modern cities. But Japan, subject to the same kinds of pressures as other developed countries, has so far maintained the centrality of the *ie*, or family clan. Indeed, as Chie Nakane claims, in essence the *ie* is not limited to relations among blood relatives, but represents a "corporate residential group . . . a managing body."[17] The Japanese are well known for having transferred their emotional loyalties to the corporation or other employment centers. The workplace substitutes for the family where that institution has eroded, and it is an extension of the family where it is intact. The words "corporate" and "managerial" suggest a rationality that obscures the deep emotional attachments involved.

At the heart of the Japanese group consciousness is the tradition of avoiding direct confrontation, of maintaining *wa*, of avoiding actions that seriously threaten the solidarity of the group. Obviously, this is not always possible, but it is the ideal: it is the equivalent in interpersonal relations to the concept of harmony with nature regarding the physical environment. Japanese politeness is part of the effort to maintain *wa*. The French journalist Jean-Claude Courdy says of the Japanese: "*Wa*, harmony, seems to be the supreme commandment of social conduct and is linked to the concept of *ma*, the sense of space, making itself felt on the intellectual plane in a conception of time that is reckoned not in minutes or seconds but in intervals between two sounds or events."[18]

Minutes or seconds are abstract concepts without sensation. The ticking of a clock is a sound and an event. In the experience of living, harmony requires continual adjustment to changing sounds, shapes, and events. But life, of course, is not always harmonious—no matter what philosophy is followed. This reality must also be adjusted to.

During the war it was a source of puzzled contempt for Americans that the Japanese would fight to the death in hopeless situations rather than surrender, which the Japanese considered to be dishonorable. We did not consider it dishonorable to surrender when there was no chance of getting away alive, provided that as prisoners we did not give away information that would endanger our own people and cause. But when the Japanese soldiers were captured, most of them would talk freely, trying to be "good prisoners." The situation of being a soldier for them seemed to be separate from that of being a prisoner. When they found themselves in such an unplanned situation, it called forth a different kind of behavior, although they were consistent with their culture in bowing to established authority, which in the new situation was represented by American guards. (I presume this was also the case in other Allied armies in the Pacific war.) For us, being a prisoner was simply an abstract extension of fighting, requiring not obedience to our captors but defiance. At least some of the cruelties inflicted on Americans and their allies in Japanese prisons have been attributed to the fact that the Japanese simply could not understand their prisoners' attitude. Following the contemptible act of surrendering, this attitude seemed to offer only gratuitous and unexplainable personal insults, which the Japanese could not abide.[19]

When the bitter war ended, and we went into Japan as occupying soldiers, we had expected them to defend their land to the last man, woman, and child as they had Okinawa (and as they undoubtedly would have if the emperor had not ordered their surrender). We were dumbfounded to be treated as honored guests. We thought that this was hypocrisy. Yet in time we learned that this was not the case at all. Japan accepted the new circumstance of being an occupied country and went about realistically learning as much as possible from it. In admirably rational ways they immediately began to reevaluate their world and to remodel it. I was privileged to observe how they redesigned their own society as they later would redesign cars and computers, copying what they wanted from the West, but not exactly, and doing things their way even in the face of American military edicts. They were wide open to change, as more than one Japanese explained to me at the time, simply because the old system had not worked. Many of them knew all along that it had not been working.

Richard Minear has translated a remarkable piece of Japanese literature from World War II, the long Homeric poem *Requiem for Battleship Yamato*, by Mitsuru Yoshida. Yoshida was a young officer on the *Yamato*, the largest battleship ever to float on the oceans of the world up to that time. The *Yamato* carried a crew of more than three thousand men on a totally futile kamikaze mission during the battle of Okinawa. Yoshida was one of a bare handful to survive. He describes an intense but wholly disciplined discussion on the bridge as follows:

Against this sharp contention that the mission is doomed to fail, chief officer of the watch Lieutenant Usubuchi (chief of the first wardroom), binoculars fixed on the sea at dusk, speaks in a low voice, almost a whisper:

"The side which makes no progress never wins. To lose and be brought to one's senses: that is the supreme path. . . .

"We will lead the way. We will die as harbingers of Japan's new life. That's where our real satisfaction lies, isn't it?"[20]

Surely such an outlook on life and death offers as much invincibility and immortality as is allowed any individual or culture in this world.

Science requires bridges over the intervals of awareness that only abstract thought can provide, but when it comes to art, the particularness of sensual emotional feeling must be primary. In his poem, Yoshida did what the Japanese as a people do best: he turned the dreadful and largely ugly events of the moment into transcendent art. Carl Sagan explores MacLean's brain theory in his book *The Dragons of Eden* and suggests that when we dream we see the world as mammals see it, full of vivid emotional images without logical connections.[21] Or, as some psychiatrists might say, connected by a different kind of logic. Things in dreams simply happen. The true artist gives rational order to these private images so that others can comprehend and identify with them. In essence, good art fixes in space and time the floating realities of dreams, integrated by conceptual thought, allowing us, as we do in our dreams but in a more disciplined manner, to explore realities that lie deeper than reason can penetrate.

In the pages that follow, I explore with words and photographs the way the Japanese perform what the art critic Robert Hughes aptly calls "the art of all they do,"[22] as it appears in their urban cityscapes and their green public landscapes.

4 • Urban Public Space

Japan is an island nation, and as such its outer walls are water edges. Like house walls and garden walls, these have ports of exit and entry. For two centuries before the Meiji Restoration in the mid-nineteenth century, these seaport gates were kept tightly closed, but when they were opened they permitted an inflow of ideas, actions, and actors that is perhaps without parallel in human history. And yet, the Japanese have not been culturally swamped in the process.

Japan has never been successfully invaded and conquered in all of its recorded history. It has been penetrated but never dominated. In 1945, after the failure of its greatest attempt to conquer others, it was nominally defeated but remained psychologically impregnable. That the American occupation did not exert more control in the long run may have been partly due to Japan's luck in losing militarily in that short interlude between World War II and the Cold War. In that brief span of time, more than one erstwhile enemy became an ally. But Japan's invulnerability is probably due to its peculiar understanding of that which is most unconquerable in the human spirit.

This unconquerable human spirit appears in all peoples and is both protected and liberated by the sense of "inward orientation" described by Kurokawa. This sense, I believe, is seated in the old emotional limbic system that is literally *within* the biologically modern human brain. It is in those interior mental regions, in my hypothesis, that the ineffable sense of a presence that we call *spirit* originates, and that is why science has so much trouble accommodating religion. Nevertheless, the capacity to "see the invisible expanse of nature through solid masonry walls," which Kurokawa conjures up, can be given physical expression in architecture by means of the abstract thought processes of the outer cortex, the logical "thinking cap." An inward sense of place, of course, does not pertain only to the home space, in Japan or anywhere else, but can include the entire homeland and sometimes much more territory. But it is an extension of the feeling for personal home, and it is always bounded in one way or another. The conceptualizing parts of the brain, however, can see beyond water edges or other territorial boundaries at least as easily as through concrete walls. The inner world of feeling, being older in an evolutionary

sense, is therefore more basic to nature as a whole than the world of abstract concepts. It is thus the most fundamental of the two planes of experience and must be protected in order for the entire human brain to be sufficiently relaxed to open itself up to the limitless vistas made possible by our rational faculties. What happens when this protection is not granted is that the abstractions become appropriated, territorialized, by the inner emotional brain, and the concepts become fanaticism instead of science.

If this is true, then it is the very insularity of the Japanese island-nation through the centuries that has enabled it to be so receptive to ideas from India, China, and Korea long before it rather precipitously began to learn from the cultures we lump together as the West. Indeed, it is interesting to consider that so many other societies that have spearheaded rapid advances in civilization have been islands or peninsulas, like those of the Mediterranean or Britain.

The ambivalent effect of Japan's psychological boundaries on visitors has been noted by many observers, and I quote in a roundabout way a phrase identified with three prominent American writers on Japan: Donald Richie attributes to former U.S. ambassador Edwin O. Reischauer the term "Seidensticker Syndrome," referring to Edward Seidensticker's evocation of the vacillating love-hate feeling foreigners often come to have for the Japanese when trying to live with them.[1] Jean-Claude Courdy did not use that term, but he refers to the experience in some detail,[2] as did my father in his time.

The love-hate response of people to any foreign place, I imagine, derives also from our evolutionary origins. When other mammals meet strange members of their own species, there is usually a good deal of huffing and puffing, of sniffing and prowling cautiously about, of signals and countersignals, until all concerned figure out their social status in the territory. Human cultures have evolved varied and elaborate ways of expressing, coping with, covering up, or neutralizing territorial propensities. Hospitality and xenophobia express opposite responses to strangers, who provide the stimulation of novelty but also are a potential threat to security.

The visitor to Japan has the sense that all human experience is intensified there, including both hospitality and xenophobia. This ambiguous intensity could be at the root of the Seidensticker Syndrome.

The visitor feels like a highly honored guest much of the time but is constantly aware of being a guest.

Before looking at how this works out in Japanese public places, let us consider again in more detail the underlying human phenomenon. The psychoanalyst and psychohistorian Erik Erikson reasons that because human infants are born into the world so helpless and require a long period of intensive parental care, our evolution required that the young be bound firmly to their native group and the place it inhabits in order to assure that they would learn its ways of survival. He calls that "pseudospecies," the compulsion of human beings to identify themselves not as human beings but as members of a tribe in a tribal territory and to define being human in terms of the culture of their tribe, to respond to the tribe as other animals do to their species.[3]

Our emotional life is intimately bound up with territorial and social ranking impulses. Our conceptualizing imagination, however, leads many of us to want to break out of the confines of tribal tradition, and it is mostly when that occurs that cultural (and technical) developments emerge. In my view, cultural evolution occurs mainly at the traditionally unbounded scale in which human beings can interact as members of the human species, rather than as members of a tribe. This scale of experience is made possible by abstract thought working out through the common symbols of human neurophysiology.

For the complex array of tribal uses of space that human beings exhibit, I have adapted the word *proxemic* coined by the anthropologist Edward T. Hall to designate the study of the human use of space specifically as an expression of local culture.[4] To match it, I have invented the term *distemic* to describe the use of space for the more impersonal, abstract relationships that enable members of various social groups to deal with each other amicably. This word is intended to suggest both greater social distance and larger physical scale.[5] *Proxemic* as I use the word is quite close in meaning to the adjective *tribal*, but proxemic relationships can be very modern, as in a professional society, a scientific discipline, a trendy youth culture or a Japanese corporation. They include those values, myths, and rituals that bind together citizens of a modern nation, as well as the more ancient traditions that the word *tribal* usually signifies. What I mean by *distemic* is very close to

cosmopolitan, but all sorts of industrial relationships and places, such as a large factory or an airport, can be distemic without being what most of us think of as cosmopolitan. I would include an American corporation in this latter category.

I like to think of distemic space as the worldwide locale of a community of strangers. By contrast, proxemic space is the territory of the pseudospecies. Distemic space is not, strictly speaking, a territory at all, if we use the ethological definition of territory as a defended space, since the function of distemic space is to be freely accessible to all who do not interfere with the rights of others. But it is a community in the sense that those who use it for civilized purposes, as a center or forum for social diversity, have a common interest in keeping it usable and safe. This is achieved by relatively arbitrary and abstract laws. At best, these laws permit a community based on common humanity. It is in distemic space that we meet as human beings, not primarily as members of a tribe.

It is easy for modern urban people to idealize proxemic village life and to overlook the fact that the price of mutual support offered by a close community is a good deal of meddling. In such communities, interpersonal conflicts can be hard to escape. Even Yukio Mishima, who was so enamored of ancient Japanese traditions that he committed ritual suicide to reassert them, knew this. In his lyric love story *The Sound of Waves*, although things eventually turn out well, he nevertheless shows how oppressive local gossip can be and how the ablest youth of an island community reach out to a larger world.[6] At least for some people of all ages, there is a special kind of delight in roaming freely in a public place, surrounded by human beings with whom one is not personally involved. Under such circumstances, free of threat to one's own ego, where status and achievement are irrelevant, one can really see humanity as a part of nature.

In design terms, the intricacies, the natural variety, the subtleties and ambiguities of form that are possible in proxemic neighborhood environments are practical because those who use these places regularly can be expected to know them well or to have local friends or relatives who know them well. These qualities are what make neighborhood environments sensually and emotionally interesting to residents and strangers alike. But such places can also be highly confusing to strangers, and sometimes the small scale, while reassuring, can also be confining. In distemic spaces, clarity and legibility are important,[7] and at best they are achieved without monotony. Landmarks must convey recognizable and meaningful symbols to strangers, often through abstract forms. These forms must call forth universal human responses to the environment.

It is the Japanese insistence on putting closed boundaries around many aspects of their proxemic life that causes problems for foreigners. All peoples do this to some extent, but like everything else, the Japanese do it in more carefully explicit ways than other cultures. And yet, Japan is unusually hospitable to foreigners and foreign ideas. This can be flattering to strangers, but the hospitality of the Japanese has clear limits, and unless one knows them very well, it is confined to particular contexts. The continual awareness of worlds one cannot enter because one does not know the proper rituals makes the foreigner feel very, very foreign, more so, reportedly, than visitors feel in America, where we have a society created in the process of assimilating successive waves of strangers. But the price of this American openness to strangers is that we presume that everyone else is—or ought to be—just like Americans. The Japanese do not expect, and probably do not want, anyone else to be like the Japanese. By putting explicit boundaries on their social territories, the Japanese accommodate differences that tend to be threatening to Americans. The Japanese hold fast to carefully orchestrated similarities in those contexts where psychological security matters most and leave themselves free to experiment in domains where unpredictability does not threaten psychological well-being. At least that is my hypothesis.

I have observed three aspects to this social-spatial pattern in the Japanese cultural landscape. First, there are the walls or boundaries that separate the private physical spaces from the public ones, as discussed in chapter 2, so that the home, no matter how cramped, becomes a place of retreat from the uncertainties of public life without becoming a prison. Second, the concept of the *ie* as a functional unit enables the Japanese to transfer domestic proxemic relationships to situations such as the workplace, which in the West are likely to be more impersonal and distemic.

The walls they place around both private and public spaces separate each set of relationships with its stresses and strains, its excitements and possibilities and threats from any other, making each of these manageable in its own frame.

Third, there are those legendary Japanese manners, those rituals that accompany every Japanese activity and tend to be special to each situation. Manners as carefully modulated as those of the Japanese can be thought of as a form of art: behavioral art. Of course, the Japanese are quite capable of being rude in situations where they consider rudeness appropriate, but their rudeness seems quite unlike the merely careless rudeness one so often finds in America. Indeed, even their rudeness can be considered a negative aspect of "the art of all they do."

Manners can be thought of as a way of placing behavioral boundaries or walls around social spaces and as gateways to communication. Like the fences around homes, the polite formalities of Japanese society can exclude foreigners from some situations while making them feel quite at home in others. Many of the rituals are unique to the culture: for example, there are subtle differences in the length and character of a bow appropriate to each person. But other aspects of Japanese courtesy involve especially gracious expressions of universally recognized human gestures and body language, which make the foreigner feel both important and welcome, even when he suspects that they cover up as much as they reveal. In the West, and particularly in America, where behavioral as well as physical fences are often considered rude, people cling to clichés—extremely simple and simpleminded manners and mannerisms that accommodate anyone from anywhere, but which leave the mind full of anxiety about any perception or state of being or feeling that is too complex to be encompassed by such easy formalities.

It is these three dimensions of the Japanese social landscape that in my view enable the Japanese to separate the proxemic and distemic domains, freeing each to serve its own psychic purposes, and yet, because there are connections across the boundaries as there are in the human brain itself, one is allowed to interact creatively with the other.

Tokyo

Of all the Japanese cities I have visited, Tokyo is the most distemic. But it is also highly proxemic. It has long been observed that this great sprawling metropolis is basically a collection of villages, which is probably true of any large city, at least any vital, interesting one. Herbert Gans has coined the phrase "urban villagers" to describe a now-extinct Italian ethnic community in Boston, Massachusetts. He observed that the residents maintained many of the social characteristics of small rural society in the heart of a great city.[8] Since then, the phenomenon has been observed in many places; perhaps it can be found in all cities. But, as with so many other human characteristics, in Japan it is more explicitly apparent.

Trying to find one's way around Tokyo outside of the main commercial centers and corridors is like being lost in the woods. One has to look for all sorts of cryptic signs, most of which are readily apparent only to the local inhabitants. I have been told that even natives of Tokyo get lost in Tokyo. Taxi drivers certainly do; I can testify to that. Houses and other buildings traditionally had no ordered street numbers, but were identified by the year in which they were built. A house is typically located within a neighborhood as a point in that space, not on a linear string along a street as in the West. One literally has to navigate from point to point. In the 1960s, extensive redistricting and street improvement plans were carried out,[9] but most of the city is still confusing to the stranger. This is proxemic Tokyo, which is everywhere within the metropolitan area, even at the center.

However, Tokyo is one of the world's major cities, in parts very cosmopolitan, full of strangers who are treated remarkably well. The present city of Tokyo was originally called Edo, founded by the Tokugawa shoguns in the early seventeenth century as an alternative capital to Kyoto, where the emperor remained without much power for two and a half centuries until the Meiji Restoration in 1868. In order to cement their authority and to keep an eye on the feudal lords who controlled various subsidiary domains, the Tokugawa rulers required the lords to spend part of each year in Edo, leaving their families there as hostages when they returned home.

These lords, the *daimyo*, brought with them the *samurai* and other retainers, who were followed by farmers, artisans, and merchants to service them. The service class usually left *their* families home, so Edo was populated by a floating population of relative strangers and from its very beginning could be considered to have been a cosmopolitan city and a distemic place as compared with the local towns and villages from which its inhabitants came. Yuichiro Kojiro says, "The samurai who came to Edo from all over Japan never created a new Edo culture of their own. They merely coexisted with the rest of the population, bringing to Edo and displaying there the characteristics of their provinces."[10]

The daimyo and the samurai retained their own proxemic spaces, as aristocrats tend to do anywhere. But the rest of the population formed a distemic group in their own part of the city, which in time evolved a special Edo culture, and this I believe is one of the functions of distemic relationships: to create social hybrids that lead to new proxemic entities. The major actors in this process were the members of the merchant class, which in feudal Japan had very low social status but often accumulated considerable wealth. The commercial middle class tends to be the most distemic portion of any population because the fluidity of its activities often transcends local boundaries.[11]

Modern Tokyo is very unlike Edo. The change, at the time of the Meiji Restoration, was lamented by the cosmopolites who were called Edokko. But the basic spatial divisions remain. Not only are the home spaces clearly separated from public spaces, but there are distinct separations between various kinds of proxemic neighborhood spaces and various kinds of distemic places. Tokyo as a city, however, seems to have no boundaries at all but spreads out into a mosaic of districts and suburbs. As Kojiro notes, Edo was "The City on the Plain,"[12] contained only on the east by Tokyo Bay and spreading otherwise toward the distant mountains. This can be considered a physical metaphor for the idea that the distemic community of strangers occupies space but has no closed boundaries. Donald Richie says of Tokyo's unique streetscape:

What is enclosed is, thus, private property. And what is open is not—it is public. So it is with most Western cities as well. But in Japan the difference is that the public space appears to belong to no one. . . . Therefore the streets of Tokyo are allowed an organic life of their own. They grow, proliferate, and on all sides street life takes on unrestricted natural forms. . . . The significance of public areas belonging to no one is not that they belong to everyone but that they can be used by just about anyone. This means that the owners or leasees of private land can be as idiosyncratic as they like.[13]

This is as good a description as I have ever read of what I mean by *distemic*, and Tokyo is as good an example of the concept as I have ever seen. I did not expect to find it to be such a good example when I first returned to Japan, having heard so much of Japan's insularity, and I was astonished at the effect Tokyo had on me.

The foreign cognoscenti of Japan will tell visitors who frequent the distemic parts of Tokyo that they never see the "real Japan." This is true, of course, depending on your definition of what is real. Almost everyone in any country deplores tourists when not actually engaged in being one himself or profiting from their presence. Although tourists do indeed wreak cultural havoc with interesting places, I like to think that tourism at its best is one of the more benign and creative of distemic activities. There are, of course, many different kinds of tourists. Some travel with open eyes and open minds, seeking understanding as well as stimulation. Others see mostly what they left at home, finding escape from the restrictions and responsibilities of daily life with groups of their own kind in safe and superficially exotic surroundings. The Japanese themselves are notorious for being that sort of tourist. But so are Americans. Such tourists come from everywhere.

It is difficult for the tourist to experience firsthand the daily life of local residents in Japan, more so than in many other countries. Out of sight behind tree-topped fences under gray tile roofs, as well as in the side streets off the Ginza itself, is not only the private life, but also much of the richly ritualized public life of local restaurants, drinking places, street festivals, and other entertainments. One of the reasons I have constructed my proxemic-distemic equation is that in the West—and especially in America—we have a grossly oversimplified view of private-public relationships. We make little

distinction between the privacy of persons and the privacy of groups (cultures) vis-à-vis neighboring groups. In the neighborhoods we find *proxemic public life*, which is more public than home life but still bound by local traditions in a way that distemic or cosmopolitan life is not. In America, public spaces reserved for particular groups have increasingly become illegal as "discriminatory." One consequence of this is that local minority cultures are increasingly transposed to the distemic institutions of the larger society, which is obligated to provide a kind of token menu for various interest groups without regard to actual populations in real territories. In Japan, there is a rich mosaic of proxemic public places, each based in a local community.

In contrast to local, proxemic public spaces, where the primary activities express the special values, traditions, customs, and rituals of people whose ways are familiar to each other, are the cosmopolitan, distemic places, where free access to all comers who are not dangerous to others is the rule. It is just such places that are most satisfactory to tour-group tourists, as well as the expense-account tribes, accommodating them with the least stress on the local population. The sophisticated traveler in search of regional variety may deplore the visual cliché and commercial standardization of such places, but those are the chief characteristics that make them not only intelligible to hordes of strangers, but tolerable for people far from home.

Modern, commercial Japan, in Tokyo and elsewhere, is marvelous because it accommodates tourists so well, in such style. I believe it does that precisely because it keeps so much of its proxemic culture to itself. Travel writers often point out that one really cannot find the interesting bistros and the legendary bars, either in the Ginza or in the urban villages and village suburbs, unless one is led there by a Japanese friend who knows the local social terrain. That is just fine with me. I am prepared to take the trouble to make Japanese friends (not hard to do) or be excluded. The contrived, self-conscious folk places so sought after by tourists in America and Europe are too often neither one thing nor the other. As with other natural systems, the ecological integrity of native culture must be protected in order to let it live on its own terms, free from trampling alien feet. But the other side of the coin is that any society that totally excludes foreign influences from its national life, as Japan did for two centuries, condemns itself to economic privation and cultural stagnation. Since the Meiji Restoration, except for the fifteen years that led to and included World War II, the Japanese have learned how to exclude without isolating themselves from distemic global society. I think that they have succeeded so well because life for the Japanese is an art, the art of placing edges around space and time in both the private and the public spheres.

Robert Hughes observes, "Nowhere else in today's world, a visitor feels after the first anarchic impact of Tokyo has settled, is there a more intelligent consciousness of design than in Japan."[14] This intelligent consciousness of design might be called the *art of the particular*. In the streetscape of Tokyo and elsewhere in Japan, this particularity shows up in the idiosyncratic structures and activities cited by Richie. It does so despite the fact that so much of central Tokyo is conspicuously modern and post-modern. The great difference between Japanese modernism in architecture and most of the genre found elsewhere is in the texture of building facades at street level (72, 73). This texture is created partly by surface decoration—signs, lanterns, sculptured

72

73

objects, potted plants—but great attention is given to threshold subspaces. Public places such as restaurants often have gates, or screens, or narrow entrance corridors like those of private houses, but many others have the ubiquitous strips of hanging cloth called *noren*, which are more easily penetrated than a foyer with doors but still serve to give one the sense of entering another zone. And many if not most restaurants and places for intimate public gathering have the traditional raised floors like those in homes. However, some of the more distemic commercial establishments act as extensions of the street itself, as in bazaars and street markets the world over.

All this visual and spatial variety and texture is not necessarily put there by the architects. Some architects are reported to complain bitterly about the signs and other embellishments that cover up their buildings, but the streetscape is better for them. Right off the glossy main avenues of the Ginza, in the side streets, one finds not only bistros and richly sensuous boutique shops, but an immense variety of small shops, manufacturing establishments (74), and quite unstandardized fast-food places, where in a quite delightful way the stranger will be an object of unabashed interest to the proprietors (75). In the Tsukiji area on the bay at the eastern end of Ginza, there is the huge fish market near the site of the gracious ghetto where foreigners were confined

during the early years of the Meiji era (76). But even in sleek high-rise Shinjuku, a McDonald's has variety in its surfaces and delightful courtesy in its service that go a long way to make up for the mediocrity of the meat (77). Next to the giant sophisticated department stores, and on each side of the Keio Plaza pedestrian way, entire streets of bazaars sell the latest high-tech playthings (78). Storekeepers have time and space for chatting with residential neighbors in the late evening (79), and uniformed school children will greet the tourist in the daytime (80). At night, next to and below the great convention hotels, the street looks like an electrified fairyland (81), always Japanese but never monotonously so. How do they manage such endless variety with modern engineering?

80

81

Even the International School architecture in Japan (which it is fashionable to deplore as betraying Japanese values because it is currently unfashionable in the West) is somehow more particular to its setting than anywhere else that I have seen it. The most important aspects of modernism in architecture have been in Japan all along. Frank Lloyd Wright, among others, incorporated them into his buildings in America, and that was one of the routes by which they arrived in Europe when Wright was still largely ignored in his own country. They were thus absorbed by the European Bauhaus pioneers who returned them to America in revised form. In Japan they simply stayed home. Modular design, the essence of the International School, is also the essence not only of Japanese design, but also of Japanese thought. Modules are units of time-space.

Likewise, Japanese design has contributed to the return to decoration that has come to characterize the hodgepodge of styles known as postmodernism. That term is in my view as empty of sense (and tense) as some of the buildings erected in its name. But the sensuality that is the great contribution of the best of this movement is, as noted, natively Japanese. Of course, many of the architects of Japanese postmodernism and pastmodernism have been as mesmerized by the international abstractions of architectural theory as their Western colleagues and have set these intellectualizations in ponderous edifices of concrete, steel, and glass in central Tokyo and elsewhere. The postwar movement known as Metabolist was pioneered by Japanese architects such as Kenzo Tange. But their formalistic constructions are not able to completely escape the spirit of their own place, and of course the intention of Tange and others was not to escape but to recast that spirit.

In recent decades, these architects and their engineers feel confident that they have found ways to build earthquakeproof skyscrapers (82). As in San Francisco, Tokyo awaits the next earthquake to find out if they are right. The generally low profile of the city makes the skyscraper appear more distinctive than in those cities where tall buildings predominate. In places like Ginza, there is exuberance, color, variety and whimsy on their surfaces not typical of high-rise architecture outside of Japan (83). The tapestry of billboards and posters with that graceful ideographic script lends texture and color even to the hardest, coldest modernist buildings.

Of course, not all Japanese design is good; the worst is possibly as bad as anywhere else, depending on your point of view. Lots of the worst as well as the best can be found at bargain basement prices in the Akihabara, the twenty-block-wide electrical appliance bazaar northeast of the Imperial Palace. For my taste, not the worst but far from the best in architecture is to be found in the New Imperial Hotel at the western end of the Ginza, facing Hibiya Park just south of the Imperial Palace on the site of the old Imperial Hotel, which had been designed by Frank Lloyd Wright. Wright's famous handiwork had incorporated Japanese proxemics into his own private vision to produce a uniquely distemic place. It was also an experiment in structural technology that enabled it to withstand the earthquake of 1923. But it could not withstand the economic tidal wave that has swept over postwar Tokyo. What Wright said at the time he was designing his Imperial Hotel in 1923 can be said of that hotel's replacement by the new one in 1968: "Japanese culture has met with Occidental Architecture as a beautiful work of art might meet a terrible accident."[15] For me, the present Imperial Hotel is pleasantly posh but in appearance has little to do with Tokyo or Japan, despite a raked gravel garden at its entrance. It is not even dramatically tall, like Shinjuku's Keio Plaza Hotel. Wright's bar, however, with its hall of hexagons, has been retained on the new mezzanine (84).

The curious thing about Tokyo to the foreigner is that despite a cityscape that appears confused, incremental, haphazard, and serendipitous, everything seems to function so efficiently. I found the central area and certain key outlying nodes easy to

84

get around in and easy to find, even though I had no knowledge of the language. A major aid is the subway network, that most distemic and abstract of transportation systems. In any subway you cannot see or hear or smell anything of the environment you are passing below; all destinations are abstracted from surrounding and interconnecting spaces, so that you must follow formal codes, as does an airplane pilot flying between radio beacons above the clouds. Nevertheless, Japanese proxemics are very much present in Tokyo's stations through the shops, the advertising posters, and the people themselves. On the trains, many people sit with their eyes closed. I commented to a friend that they must be tired from the hard work and after-hours socializing for which the Japanese are known, but my friend said that they were not sleeping. He told me that they close their eyes to avoid unwanted eye contact: one of the many ways the Japanese deal with crowding. It is yet another way of putting boundaries around relationships.

Vehicular transportation routes, like pedestrian streets, constitute a basic kind of distemic space in any country, and they are even more open ended than sidewalks. It is to characterize such spaces that I have invented the word distemic. We would not call most of such spaces cosmopolitan—some sidewalks, perhaps, but hardly expressways. Anyone with the price of a ticket can ride trains or buses, regardless of manners or appearance. Anyone with

a driver's license willing to follow a few simple rules can use auto highways, regardless of other sorts of behavior. Even bank robbers in a getaway car will obey basic traffic laws, such as driving on the proper side of the road, because it is impossible to travel far without doing so. Circulation systems are the basic form-giver of cities the world over, and the street patterns remain remarkably permanent despite the movement of history. Many of the great cities of Europe began as military outposts on the roads that linked the Roman Empire. Some of the main avenues of downtown Tokyo are the terminal ends of the old Tokaido highway to Kyoto and other overland routes that brought the retinues of the daimyo to Edo. Now the celebrated Shinkansen train to Kyoto follows the Tokaido route, starting at the central Tokyo Station. At the city center, streets lie alongside of the spiral system of moats that still define the Imperial Palace grounds (85, 86), or follow filled portions, and one part of a raised expressway is built over the moat where water still flows (87).

A quarter of a century ago, Kevin Lynch identified "legibility" as the main factor in making an urban place memorable and satisfying. He was considering mainly the distemic aspects of urban form and for this purpose identified five elements that contribute to legibility: edges, paths, nodes, districts, and landmarks.[16] As we have seen, much of proxemic

85
86

87

Tokyo is low-rise and sprawling, quite illegible to strangers, but the major paths are strong. The Tokyo subway and surface rail transit system is one of the most efficient and attractive in the world. A color-coded map, clearly visible on trains and in stations and available everywhere in pocket size, as with most subways, directs you to connections. You can follow this formal, simple, worldwide language even if you do not read Japanese, if you can identify key target areas. Most of those are identified in English. Major surface streets are not that easy to follow but are manageable with a map.

Writers often remark on the phenomenon Richie refers to, that the Japanese do not feel personally responsible for public streets and other spaces outside their private walls. Several have described Japanese streets and public places as dirty and unkempt as a consequence. My father deplored this in 1918. All I can say is that I have not seen it. When I first arrived in Japan in 1945, I saw cleanliness even in the raked-up rubble of bombed buildings. Japan's public spaces seem to me to be remarkably tidy and well cared for. This may be the result of the work ethic operating in whatever agencies are officially responsible for cleanup, but one also sees what I presume to be housekeepers washing down the streets in a manner reminiscent of Dutch towns (88). Compared with New York streets and subways, Tokyo's are immaculate. Japanese drivers are aggressive and intense, but they are as well mannered in their cars as they are on foot, and one rarely sees rust or a battered fender. As for crime, the scourge of distemic places, there is of course crime in Japan, but as noted, there is little of the common street variety. Some sort of public consensus about what is permissible and what is not must be very strong. Indeed, as Jane Jacobs noted twenty-five years ago, the presence of inhabitants of strong proxemic neighborhoods is the best resource for keeping distemic streets safe for strangers.[17]

Although Tokyo is jammed with cars, most of the population rides the trains. Major urban nodes that constitute subcities have emerged around the great rail terminals like Shinjuku or Ueno, as have many of the major suburbs, just as the suburban centers of car-oriented America have grown up around Interstate Highway interchanges since World War II. But in Tokyo there is far more variety

between these subcenters than is usually found in America. Each has its proxemic qualities, which lend uniqueness and vitality to distemic places. Mostly low-rise Tokyo is full of landmarks, although one has to look for them. They do not stand out of the streetscape as in Western cities. Nevertheless, each of the major nodes on the subway and surface rail system is distinctive and memorable.

On Shibuya plaza, the most important landmark is a modest statue of the dog Hachiko, which is a popular meeting place. The life-sized bronze figure of the dog sits patiently on its blocky pedestal, its head just high enough to be seen in a crowd, near a fountain pool outside the railroad station (89). Often wearing a colorful garland, it commemorates the faithful animal that continued to meet his master's train for years after the master died, until the end of its own life. Near the statue are large posters eulogizing this species for its loyalty and obedience, those most prominent of Japanese virtues (90). The plaza is dotted with peaked, tentlike structures for patient humans to wait under in the frequently inclement weather (91).

92

In contrast to this older node is Shinjuku, until after World War II a western gateway suburb and now a major urban center, probably Tokyo's busiest traffic junction. It is a city within a city, with sleek high-rise buildings surrounding a large railroad station (92). Alongside the station, connecting with two huge department stores and numerous other enterprises and a double-level station square, is a vast underground concourse (93). Outside, a pedestrian plaza leads to the towering Keio Plaza Hotel. From a cocktail lounge on that hotel's top floor at night, one looks out on a blazing city of Oz. Beyond the station is a modern version of the old "pleasure quarters" (94, 95).

93

94

95

96

Still another major node is Ueno Station, surrounded on three sides by a commercial center and on the fourth by Ueno Park, which will be discussed in more detail in the next chapter. A lesser node is Roppongi, home of embassies and international yuppie nightlife. But perhaps the main center of Tokyo, although fully visible only from above, is the Imperial Palace. The palace itself is obscured within its moat and green grounds. The most prominent structures to be seen from surrounding streets and public parks are a gatehouse and the great concave fortress wall rising above the moat. However, to the perceptive and reasonably well informed visitor, the palace is very much *there*. Across from the grounds of the former outer moat, which now serve as a public park, stand the International School buildings of the Marunouchi district. This area used to be called the Mitsubishi Meadows. In Meiji times the meadows were owned by the financially hard-pressed army, which offered

to sell them to the emperor, but the royal household was even worse off financially. Instead the meadows were acquired by the still highly solvent Mitsubishi company.[18] It is currently one of Tokyo's most prestigious office centers (96).

Despite all the changes there in the past century, Tokyo's major districts follow the proxemic and distemic divisions of the original Edo castle city, which have been described in charming detail by Edward Seidensticker in his wistful and satiric book, *Low City, High City*.[19] In these spatial divisions, as so often happens with cities, topographic changes signal social boundaries. The district of Edo known as the *Yamanote*, which Seidensticker calls the High City, is the hilly area surrounding the castle, mainly to the south and west. This is where the daimyo and the samurai lived, and it is now the site of government buildings, embassies, big hotels, and the like. The *Shitamachi* (Seidensticker's Low City) was the flat alluvial plain lying east of the castle toward Tokyo Bay. It is laced with canals that are connected to the spiral castle moats and by the Sumida River flowing in from the north. This was the area settled by the merchants and artisans who serviced the castle aristocrats, and it contained the markets and the pleasure quarters, centered between two bridges. It was the focus of the urban landscape immortalized in Hiroshige's woodcuts "One Hundred Famous Views of Edo."[20] Here the street layout is a grid with two broad intersecting avenues, one of them the old Tokaido highway from the south, the other connecting the castle with the Sumida River. Here is where the Ginza emerged as the modern section early in the Meiji era after the fire of 1872, when the newly constituted authorities decided to rebuild, Western fashion, in brick. At that time it was known as Bricktown, stylish but also damp and uncomfortable in Tokyo's humid climate.[21]

Nothing is left of the old Bricktown; today it might be called Glasstown. The major streets are lined with high-style store windows on the ground floor of tall buildings draped with brilliant neon signs. On the streets, as well as behind the shop windows, are mannequins dressed in the latest international fashions. Curiously, the mannequins mostly have Western features (97), as do many of the faces on advertising posters and billboards (98). But Japanese receptionists and elevator girls receive customers with bows suitable for a samurai. They are reportedly trained for their jobs as arduously as kabuki actors. In current urban fashion, some of the streets in Ginza are closed to auto traffic on weekends (99). But even with cars running, Tokyo is still a pedestrian's city.

97

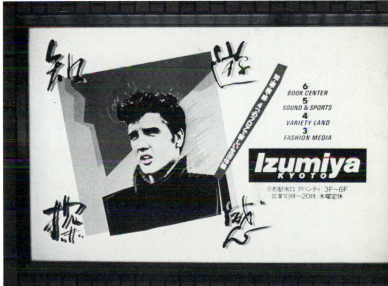

98

99

Donald Richie observes that the Tokyo street, unlike European streets and American malls, is not a stage on which people come to promenade or sit at cafes to be observed: "You, the walker, are not an actor. Rather, you are an active spectator. The display is not you and the others about you. The display is the street itself."[22] This quality of the street as spectacle is present in the Edo era woodcuts of artists like Hiroshige. The focus of street life in the Low City was then along the Sumida River, unfortunately no longer to be seen: floods were second only to fires as the leading natural disasters until they were stopped by flood control projects in the 1920s. The price of that has been visual obliteration of the once beautiful banks of the Sumida. It can now be seen only from tall buildings and bridges (100).

It was the merchant class of Edo who populated, managed, and patronized the Low City, and it was this class, in their dissatisfaction with the puritan rigidities of the shogun and the samurai, who made possible the Meiji revolution. In the Meiji era, aristocrats continued to live and conduct the nation's official business in the High City to the south and west of the Imperial Palace. They availed themselves of the attractions of the Low City, but it was not their proxemic turf.

The center of commercial and social life at that time was not in the Ginza but generally to the north of it.[23] Commercial life, of a sort, was combined with social life in the pleasure quarters, known as the Yoshiwara, the location of the most important geisha houses, tea houses, and the Japanese version of bordellos. The latter term is misleading. Prostitution (now illegal) had flourished near or even in the temples, as in the area around the Kannon Temple known as Asakusa, still a major attraction even without prostitutes. "The art of all they do" clearly applied to the pleasure quarters. Presumably the artistic formalities required of the customer mitigated some of the difficulties and indignities faced by the women who served them. I cannot speak

with authority on this subject, but in a letter from Kyoto in 1945 I described the "joro district" there as follows:

Suddenly we came to a side street that was lit up the length of its narrow pavement with round frosted bulbs in front of each stained wood house under the upturned eaves. In front of each house sat a woman in a kimono, bowing to each male passerby. Blake and I were just sightseeing, but Joe wanted to get down to business. We found a place, took off our shoes, and were escorted up small, polished, and beautifully clean stairs made of some kind of lovely blueish wood to a low front room. The room overlooked the street through a large open window from which we could see across to where our neighbors were being entertained. The walls of the room were of beautifully colored paper, with silk scrolls and prints. There was a low divan, unusual, and soft pillow-like mats around a low red lacquer table. Everything was blended so softly and tastefully that you weren't aware of the colors, of the pictures or the designs, but only of a soft reposeful atmosphere. And this was a whore-house!

A pretty girl in a bright kimono came in, bowed one of those jerky little bows and dropped softly to her knees on one of the mats. She was the entertainer. While we waited, Blake took down one of those string instruments and asked the girl to play for us. She sang us the song of the Geisha girl, a haunting plaintive melody, in a sweet almost childish voice, wavering from high to low notes. Even after Joe returned with his girl, we stayed and talked, and it was as pleasant a place to stay and talk as you could find in Kyoto to sit and talk, cross-legged on a soft mat.

Donald Richie, who seems to know Japan as well as any living foreigner, declares that the Japanese, whatever their other vices, are incapable of sordidness. It is one of the few unequivocal statements he seems willing to make about Japan.[24] In my experience he is right. During the war, I saw the results of Japanese depravity, but I have never seen anything Japanese that can be called sordid. It seems to me that sordidness derives from complete indifference to appearances. Art—all art, any art—is a matter of appearances. In art, a thing is what it appears to be; art manifests hidden reality. Being made manifest, the reality takes the form of the appearance.

One could wish that more of the Meiji Low City were apparent in modern Tokyo, along with much more of the Sumida River. In *Low City, High City*, Seidensticker describes the summer "opening of the Sumida" festival. He presents two different views of the scene through the eyes of two Americans. One of these was the large-minded Edward S. Morse:

It was a sight never to be forgotten: the men's bodies glistening in the light with the showers of sparks dropping like rain upon them, and looking back, the swarms of boats, undulating up and down, illuminated by the brilliancy of the display; the new moon gradually setting, the stars shining with unusual brightness, the river dark, though reflecting the ten thousand lantern lights of all sizes and colors, and broken into rivulets by the oscillations of the boats.[25]

The other American was the youthful daughter of a missionary family that had joined those emissaries of cultural imperialism then bringing Civilization and Enlightenment to Japan. This was the reaction of Clara Whitney:

The Sumida stretched out before us, and for nearly a mile up and down it was covered with a myriad of boats, from the clumsy canal boat to the gay little gondola dancing like a cockle shell on the tiny wavelets. . . . Millions of lanterns covered the river as far as we could see until the sober Sumida looked like a sea of sparkling light. . . . It was altogether a pretty sight—the brilliantly lighted houses, the illuminated river, the gay fireworks, and crowds of lanterns held aloft to prevent their being extinguished. . . . Like a stream of humanity they passed our perch and Mama and I spoke with sadness of their lost and hopeless condition spiritually.[26]

The final comment is the more unforgivable because the two ladies were not blind to the magic of the moment. A great-granddaughter of someone like Clara Whitney would not react exactly that way today, but might well have equally mixed feelings toward such a festival. There is a basic puritanism, I believe, that has diminished the public life of modern cities in the West. "Northwest" would be more accurate, since the public spaces of Mediterranean and Latin American countries retain much sensuality in form and action. I recall an elegant Chilean woman in Mexico City telling me, "You Americans are sensually deprived." Despite the commercial hedonism of our sexually permissive but still spiritually shriveled times, the fear of uninhibited joy and the exuberant beauty that comes with it has not vanished. To be "cool" is the emotional ideal, the old repressions appearing in new form. Having a good time in much of the West is now a logical, rational objective blessed by psychologists and sociologists, a sort of moral duty, but genuine enthusiasm and spontaneity remain very bad manners, if not mortal sins.

Richie provides an excellent description of the emotional openness of the Japanese (under the appropriate circumstances, of course):

The Japanese are a people who have managed to retain, right into the latter half of the dehumanized twentieth century, a very human, even primitive, quality: their innocence. While this does not prevent great subtlety and a degree of sophistication, this mighty innocence—one that the Japanese share with those the white man elsewhere calls natives—rests upon an uncompromising acceptance of the world as it is. The innocent does not look for reasons behind reasons. He, secure in the animal nature that all of us have and only half of us admit, is able to see that all reality is what the West finds merely ostensible reality.[27]

This kind of innocence, childlike without being childish, suffuses the Japanese urban landscape. It requires a very whole, if divided, mind. Genuine artists and scientists have it, at least in their work. In my view, the innocence comes from letting the mammalian core of the human brain function on its own terms, without inhibition from the conceptualizing outer cortex, simultaneously freeing the conceptual imagination to do what it does best. Art is the result of interconnecting the two regions of the brain in responding to particular contexts. I believe art—whether of the environment or of objects and actions within it—is the only way such connections can concretely be made.

Kyoto

Travelers to Japan, as well as some Japanese, often deplore the apparent erosion of such innocence in places like Tokyo, assuming it lives only in antiques, failing to recognize it in modern dress. Both native and foreign visitors pour into Kyoto in search of innocence in vintage form. Kyoto is a sort of living museum of historical Japan, remarkably immune not only to postmodernity and pastmodernity, but even to Meiji modernity. But Kyoto is much too alive to be called a museum. Purists complain of the impact of contemporary culture on the city, but as I have noted above, I myself have been surprised that it has changed so little, not only since the American occupation, but also since my parents' time, considering the changes that have occurred elsewhere in Japan and the world in general.

Although Kyoto is flooded with tourists from everywhere, including the rest of Japan, one suspects that they are largely kept out of the neighborhoods. At least the neighborhoods look kept out of. Still, Kyoto citizens must face the problem that they share with the towns and cities of my native New England, that of finding protection from nostalgic seekers after ancient verities in the greener grass of other people's pastures. These strangers are not content simply to snap pictures and move on. They stay around and do their best to convert what they find to what they came from, like "wilderness lovers" who bring fully equipped house trailers to the national parks.

The messiest of such émigrés are the members of the international counterculture whose proxemic code affects cynicism rather than innocence. The emotional myopia that blinds this tribe to the virtues of whatever country they have fled also blinds them to the actual—as opposed to the alleged—beauties of the place they set up in. As the landscape we all inhabit is partly composed of interior mental images, it is also the stuff that literature and drama are made of. The literature of the counterculture I have seen is particularly bleak, a tinny mirror reflecting nothing but itself. Jay McInerney's novel *Ransom* describes Kyoto from the point of view of such people who "had in common only what they had already left behind." [28] The protagonist of this story is obsessed with looking deeper than his cohorts, but he never sees what lies all around him: "When Ransom arrived he had wanted to penetrate the walls, to become intimate with whatever it was he imagined was within, behind the walls and the polite faces, something outside the conceptual frames he had inherited; he wanted to breach the appearances of the world and look into the heart of things."[29]

This is the direct opposite of the reality in appear-

101

ances that is, as Richie notes, the distinguishing characteristic of Japanese spaces and Japanese life. In McInerney's word picture of Kyoto, one of the few bits of native Japanese environment to be seen is a grungy Buddhist monastery where an émigré Oklahoma jock steals a sword with which, in an improbable ritual, he kills the tragic hero of the tale, mercifully ending it. The only thing that is finally penetrated is the seeker's own body.

In Kyoto, such types along with a multitude of other, more outward-looking strangers congregate in the general vicinity of the modern railroad plaza. There, among a few pastmodern first-class hotels, are the neither-nor second class ones. But the streetscape is nevertheless full of texture, less flamboyant than Tokyo's but still interesting (101). In its coffee shops, which are a large part of Japan's public life, a *gaijin* (foreigner) can feel welcome enough, provided he does not try to penetrate too many walls (102).

A controversial tower is the most prominent landmark in this area (103). Critics say it is all wrong as a symbol of Kyoto, and it certainly is no postmodern pagoda. Halfway to its top, on the upper floor of the hotel on which the tower stands, there is a Disneyland-type amusement center, which young Japanese flock to with enthusiasm (104). On the observation deck at the top of the tower, one can play pinball machines high in the air with one's back to a fine panoramic view of the city (105).

103   104   105

106

Unlike Tokyo, Kyoto is both legible and well bounded. It was laid out in a grid borrowed from China. It was planned as a new capital in the eighth century to take the imperial court out from under the influence of the Buddhist priests who dominated the earlier capital at Nara. The major boulevards are broad and spacious, widened as firebreaks during World War II (106). The city lies in a saucer ringed by mountains on the east, north, and west. It is bisected by the Kamo River, joined in the plain to

the south by the Katsura River, which forms an edge on Kyoto's western side. These become the Yodo River, which flows some thirty miles to Osaka Bay, linking the two cities with a riverside park we will consider in chapter 5.

Below the Kyoto Tower and the large hotel on which it sits are acres of high-priced urban land devoted to the Higashi-Honganji Temple complex (107). Within the generous white gravel yards of this temple, the stranger is welcome to join native

107

108

tourists and, if so disposed, to contemplate the contrasts in time-space (108). Kyoto has one subway, very handsome and efficient (109), which runs due north from the railroad station under broad and busy Karasuma Street. It goes past, or rather under, the outer edge of the old Imperial Palace to the region of several universities north and west of it. At the main station of the subway there is a lighted map that tells the passenger where each train is at any

moment, compensating for the claustrophobia of being underground (110). Compared with Tokyo, Kyoto is remarkably easy to find one's way around in and to stay oriented in.

But that does not keep it from being mysterious and interesting. Behind the appearances, there are other appearances. The sense of life within, as well as without, is everywhere (111). A public restaurant has the same hierarchy of spaces, the progression from outside to inside, exposure to enclosure, the garden within, described in chapter 2 in connection with traditional houses (112, 113). Private-public, proxemic-distemic relationships are a continuum in Kyoto as elsewhere in Japan. A coffee shop in the Gion entertainment district has latticed windows facing the street with opaque glass at eye level. One can see passing feet and car wheels but not faces, knowing the public is there without feeling looked in on (114). At a busy traffic intersection, the Yasaka

109

110

111

112

113

114

Shrine marks the gateway to Maruyama Park, enclosed but fully accessible, delightfully public (115). From the top of Mount Hiei at the northeastern corner of the city, the whole of Kyoto seems to be enclosed by walls of hills (116).

Within the grounds of the Yasaka Shrine where it meets Maruyama Park, a shady walled street (117) leads past narrow, textured, human-scale, infinitely varied but unified side streets (118, 119), from which you can see glimpses of courtyards and gardens (120, 121). The streets become stairs (122), lined with restaurants and gift shops as you climb toward the Kiyomizu Temple complex on the side of the Higashiyama range.

118

119

121

120

122

The great Kiyomizudera, with its soaring upturned eaves of richly carved dark wood, stands on a wide platform jutting out from the mountainside with only the rear of the building anchored in the ground (123). Nearby, a dark three-story pagoda rises out of the pine trees (124). From the platform, in the spring before the leaves are out, the city of Kyoto can be seen surrounded by its horseshoe ring of mountains, open to the plain to the south. Patches of green reveal the location of the thousand other temples and shrines in the city, the sun glinting on their red, gold, gray, and blue peaked roofs. Except for the Kyoto Tower spearing the clouds near the station, this scene is much as I remember it from the time I stood there at the age of twenty-five.

123
124

Of the Kyoto he had known in 1917 and 1918, when the guns of the first world war were still firing in Europe, my father had written: "Swept by fire and plague, wracked by conqueror and would-be conqueror . . . Kyoto has stood . . . remaining the city of beauty and peace withal . . . thanks to him who looks after real worth in life and saves it from annihilation."[30]

I was reminded of that statement by a document in the writing table of our guest apartment in the Amherst House of Doshisha University, written by Otis Cary, who had been an intelligence officer with the American occupation.[31] Cary had known what most of us did not know, that Kyoto had narrowly missed a "fiery plague" and "annihilation" just before the war's end. I was stunned to learn four decades after the fact that Kyoto had been selected as the first target for the atomic bomb that instead fell on Hiroshima. Point zero was the roundhouse in the railroad yards to the west of Kyoto Station. A diagram drawn by Cary's student at Doshisha shows the area of destruction, which would have included the Yasaka Shrine and Maruyama Park, San-jusangendo with its 3,333 images of the goddess Kwanon, the old Imperial Palace, Nijo Castle, the Gion entertainment section, and Doshisha University. The Kiyomizudera and most of what lay below it would have been gone.[32] Kyoto of a thousand years and a thousand shrines and temples would have ceased to exist.

Kyoto citizens had speculated reverently on what high-placed American might have spared their city. Many credited MacArthur with saving Kyoto and Nara from the conventional air raids that destroyed so many other Japanese cities, and apparently MacArthur made little effort to deny that. Cary notes that scholars in Kyoto favored Langdon Warner, an authority on oriental art at Harvard well known and honored in Kyoto, as having intervened with military authorities to save its art treasures. But Cary eventually established that the person solely responsible for saving Kyoto from the atom bomb was the secretary of war, Henry L. Stimson, who thought the historic city "belonged to the world." Stimson had personally and single-handedly opposed the recommendations of all the military and civilian members of the top secret Target Committee and persuaded President Truman to support him. Stimson's veto of the selection of Kyoto as a target for the atom bomb probably saved it from the final firebomb raids that would have destroyed its wooden buildings almost as effectively.[33]

Among the most visually gorgeous of the landmarks thus saved is the brilliant red and gold Heian Shrine with its three-story red torii arching over the street outside the museum in which I had been billeted in 1945. Both can be seen at the center of photo 125. A few blocks beyond them at the base of the Higashiyama range, to the far left in photo 125, is the modern bulk surrounding the old Miyako

127

128

Hotel where my mother had met my father. Adjacent to the Heian Shrine is the sacred garden where I spent many off-hours during the occupation (126). Photo 127 shows the bridge as it was in 1945. Photo 128 shows it as it is now. Time has worked its way with the vegetation, but the spirit of the place is unchanged.

As I have said, I found the spirit of Kyoto surprisingly unchanged from those early postwar days, despite the contrast in the well-being and the life-styles of its residents. Photos 129 and 130 are printed from old negatives I found among my notes of the period. Photo 131 is a contemporary picture of the interior of a hotel we frequented. It probably did not look exactly like that then, but it seems familiar. Kyoto, like other Japanese communities, has its local festivals, *matsuri,* when, notwithstanding Richie's observation, the streets become a stage and the spectators are participants. There is the cherry blossom festival in the spring and the leaf-viewing festival in the fall, but Kyoto's most exuberant festival is the Gion Matsuri. It is now held in July, but in 1918 it took place early in August. On her twenty-seventh birthday, while watching one of the festival

129 130

131

processions file past the veranda of the old Miyako Hotel, my mother met my father. In her account of the festival, her feelings seem midway between those of Edward Morse and Clara Whitney on the banks of Tokyo's Sumida River a generation before:

I saw the god emerge that hot night in Kyoto and fell for a moment under his strange enchantment. As I came through the night shadows of the Shinto grove, I saw temple-courts glowing with lanterns. . . . Suddenly there was a shout and a flare of fire. Boys sped from the temple, waving bundles of burning fagots that shed red coals and hot ashes in passing. The people stooped and gathered these coals into basins, scrambling for them like beggar boys for pennies. This . . . was to cleanse the air against the coming of the god. So at least an affable gentleman in a kimono and foreign shoes explained to me.

Even as he spoke, I heard a kind of chanting shout among the temple lanterns, and the palanquin of the god swooped from the temple on the shoulders of myriads of dancing men. Joyously he burst forth . . . like the entrance of the Bacchantes in a Greek play. Indeed, as my friend in the kimono and the foreign shoes volunteered, Bacchus, in the form of sake, had materially assisted in the jubilation and the god's release.

I don't know how it happened, but that reflection on the subject of religion and alcohol was my last conscious and detached thought in the matter of this festival. I came to, for a moment, as from a dream, to find myself part of a great swaying crowd of lanterns and scraping shoes, moving on and on through the night in the wake of that heaving palanquin; and then I forgot again. My identity, my foreign prejudices, were merged in the strong primitive force of this crowd emotion that was irresistible and causeless . . . for through it all there was a curious, passionate joy, elemental, senseless, voluptuous.

Only when we came to a halt at the river's edge and felt around us the sober outlines of the hills and the quietude of the far-off stars, did I come to as from intoxication. . . . Suddenly I felt very old, very grave, with the puritan gravity of our race which long ago transmitted the mysterious, sensuous exultation of pagan religion into moral energy. . . . In a moment, in that swift uncanny way in which crowds in Japan suddenly disappear, the scene of brilliance and excitement was snuffed out like a flame in the darkness. As I walked home, everyone seemed to be already asleep in the little grey houses, and nothing was abroad in all the city, save a lonely flute somewhere in the velvet darkness of a Shinto grove.[34]

132

Sixty-six years after she wrote that I could imagine feeling the presence of that god as I returned alone to the Gion entertainment quarter of theaters, cabarets, and geisha houses. Despite the shiny cars and modern dress of the people that now filled its spaces, the essential ambience seemed to me much as it had been when I had walked as a soldier on the Gion's soft, dim, sensually textured streets, festooned with paperlike lanterns that cast a cherry blossom tint over the latticed house fronts (132, 133). There, even in those hungry, depressed days immediately following the war, laughter drifted out on the soft yellow light from the paper-glazed windows of the woody second stories (134). Now I met three geisha who appeared like celestial apparitions in the dim street (135), much as one might meet famous actors on Broadway. Now, as then and in my mother's time, the street itself is very much the theater, and you, the walker, are the audience, enjoying vicariously the festivities behind the latticed windows of the cabarets.

Thus, a proxemic module of time-space can capture and enfold into itself visitors from the distemic community of strangers for a string of moments spread over what amounts in this case to three generations of human consciousness. Multiplied by thousands or millions, this is the sense in which the quintessentially Japanese city of Kyoto does, as Stimson declared, belong to the world.

133

135

134

Kobe

Timeless, traditional Japan, as expressed by Kyoto, needs no promotion in the community of strangers who approach it with open eyes and open hearts. Tokyo, however, presents to the stranger a dense mosaic of old and new spaces, much more confusing and controversial and yet equally, if differently, Japanese. The port city of Kobe emphasizes the new and modern in its own traditional way. Like Kyoto, it is bounded by a wall of mountains, but only on one side. On the opposite side it is edged by water like Tokyo, but its harbor is much more integrated into its city form. In the thirteenth century, when it was known as Hyogo, it was a key point on both land and water routes, and it prospered as a trading port with China for three more centuries until the Tokugawa closed Japan to the world. After the Meiji Restoration in 1868, it emerged again as a major port under the name of Kobe. In the next fifty years the population multiplied nearly ten times to a million people. The increase was in part the result of an influx of foreigners seeking trade. During the course of World War II the population was more than halved, but it currently stands at nearly a million and a half.

As its population grew on the narrow shelf of land between the mountains and the sea, development crept up the mountainsides, eventually spreading over the plateau into a number of new towns. To accommodate the continued pressure for both housing and shipping facilities, in the mid-sixties an ambitious scheme was developed called the "mountains-go-to-sea project." Over one hundred million cubic yards of earth were cut off the hills at the western end of the city and dumped in the harbor near the city center to create a new town called Port Island. The leveled land left in the mountains was then used for housing lots. Port Island was planned to be "a cultural city on the sea . . . with all the facilities necessary for the life of city people."[35] Twenty thousand people have been scheduled to live in sixty-five hundred apartments alongside of twelve container berths and sixteen liner berths, which can accommodate twenty-eight oceangoing ships at one time.

For the commercial visitor, the centerpiece of Port Island is the Portopia Hotel, which offers from its upper rooms spectacular views of the harbor. Within

136

137

138

the hotel, a serpentine river curls through the lobby, connecting an outdoor garden to an indoor lake (136). Even in that spacious, accessible public place, seats are grouped to form pleasantly restful, intimate subspaces (137). Outside in the courtyard, on the right occasion, one can watch a traditional Noh play from the surrounding galleries.

It is remarkably easy to get back and forth to the older city center. The monorail, called the Portliner, takes the visitor or commuter from Sannomiya Station four miles over a highly visible landscape of housing and office towers and containerized piers, across a bridge of bright red steel, to the postmodern city nestled under its towering hills (138). It is a landscape of great energy and considerable beauty, despite the generally dreary architecture of the island new town. Although millions of cubic yards of mountain went to sea, there is a great deal of moun-

tain left, much of it preserved in scenic parks, which will be considered in chapter 5.

The center of the old city is not unlike Tokyo's Ginza in its flamboyant postmodernism and stylish, purposeful crowds. In some respects it seems even more contemporary in style, with a greater sense of space and awareness of the surrounding environment. Next to the large Sannomiya railroad station, which is also the central city terminal of the monorail to Port Island, there is a public square, well planted with green trees, circumvented by a raised walkway (139, 140). Nearby is the central plaza shopping arcade, which extends for several blocks. Linking the central area with the harbor is a broad boulevard called Flower Road, which is lined with sculptures as well as flowers. Those traveling on the raised monorail with its expansive views of city, sea, and mountains become particularly aware of the long

139

140

town, called Rokko Island, is currently being created by fill moved from the mountains to a point in the sea just east of Port Island. It will be the largest man-made island in the world. The booster rhetoric makes it appear that contemporary Culture and Enlightenment, based on the doctrine that bigger is better, is being imported from America. But I doubt if the Japanese of Kobe really believe in bigness for its own sake.

Kobe's downtown side streets are full of intimate, playfully decorated shops, restaurants, and bars. Next to the modest hotel where I stayed was a restaurant with the front of a railroad engine embedded in its facade, as if, having inadvertently plowed through the dining room, it politely stopped for pedestrians on the street outside (141). Although this city conveys a more cosmopolitan, outward-looking, international spirit than either Tokyo or Kyoto, the boundaries that separate its proxemic and distemic zones of activity are as firm as they are elsewhere in Japan. Just off the major commercial streets of offices, hotels, and places of entertainment are gates like the one in photo 142, signaling the entrance to a low-rise, low-key residential neighborhood backed up against the mountainside.

141

harbor and its highly mechanized activities that draw on the primordial energy of the world's oceans.

The Kobe Port Coloring Coordination operation has been devised by city authorities to insure that the outer walls of sheds, warehouses, offices, and other buildings in the port area will be standardized in creamy colors, while the windows and roofs will be painted in bright colors, to indicate the ten planning zones into which the area is subdivided. Aesthetics aside, the color-coded zoned areas will be as helpful to foreigners trying to find their way around the port as are the color-coded maps of the Tokyo subway.

According to the planners, "There still exist in Kobe some areas where wooden houses dating from the prewar period cluster. Redevelopment of these areas poses one of the most important targets for city planning."[36] Some of us will lament the demise of those wooden houses; whether the people who live in them will is not indicated. A second island new

142

Sapporo

Sapporo, the capital of the Hokkaido Prefecture on the northernmost of Japan's four main islands, is modern in a different way than Kobe. This part of Japan has been settled almost entirely during the past century. Its latitudes are roughly those of America's New England states. The natural environment strikes the New Englander as very much like home, but as for the man-made landscape, the initial effect on an American arriving from Honshu is more like going from the east coast of the United States into the plains states—almost nothing made by man is more than a hundred years old. This Japanese frontier was from the outset strongly influenced by American culture, and its historic buildings are so like those of the eastern United States around the turn of the century that a Yankee visitor has an overpowering sense of déjà vu. However, the very similarity of the physical environment makes the American acutely aware of the persistence of Japanese traditions and the pervasiveness of the Japanese spirit. It is here, more than anywhere else, that one sees how independent traditional Japanese culture is from the environmental antiques with which it is commonly associated.

Ironically, the American individual who probably was most instrumental in lending Hokkaido a New England ambience is still famous throughout Japan and almost totally unknown in his own land. William S. Clark, a contemporary of Edward S. Morse, was the first sitting president of the Massachusetts Agricultural College (now the University of Massachusetts) and was also the founding president of Sapporo Agricultural College (now the University of Hokkaido). He is credited by many with being the founder of modern agriculture in Japan, although this distinction is shared by several other foreigners, mostly American, who came to Japan during the Meiji era. Today Clark's name and image can be seen throughout the Hokkaido campus and the city of Sapporo. A twenty-foot lighted photomural of a great statue of Clark, pointing grandly over a fertile valley, greets arriving passengers at Sapporo's Chitose Airport (143). On the University of Massachusetts campus in Amherst, he is known only as a name on a building, obscured by English ivy.[37]

Hokkaido was the last stronghold of the supporters of the Tokugawa shogun as they retreated across Tsugaru Strait, which separates the island from Honshu. Although this northern region had long been considered Japanese territory and was the feudal domain of the Matsumae clan on its southern tip, until the mid-nineteenth century it was populated mainly by the Ainu, an aboriginal people whose history and fate is similar to that of the American Indians. The retreating Tokugawa lords built a fort at Hakodate (now a park), but they were crushed in 1869 by a Meiji government expedition under the command of Kiyotaka Kuroda. The Meiji authorities then installed Kuroda as vice-governor of the Hokkaido Colonization Commission (Kaitakushi). Like many of the leaders of the new Japan, Kuroda went abroad to learn Western concepts of science, technology, economics, and education. According to Clark's biographer, John M. Maki, Kuroda was instrumental in the selection of Clark, a respected geologist and botanist as well as an academic administrator, to found a new college of scientific agriculture in frontier Hokkaido. Kuroda became Clark's immediate superior during Clark's stay in Japan. That stay lasted only eight months, but as a result of it, Clark's ideas and personality became indelibly imprinted on the re-

143

gion around Sapporo. Although his usefulness to
the Japanese was as a scientific pragmatist, it was his
spiritual influence on his students, many of whom
became important government leaders in later years,
that set him apart from other technical advisors from
abroad. He was a devout Christian and insisted, over
Kuroda's strong opposition, on teaching the Bible
at the new college. A number of Japanese converted
to Christianity at the time, but few seem to have
retained that faith or given it much attention. Rather,
Clark remains a symbol of the frontier spirit of individual freedom and self-reliance.[38] He is best remembered for his parting words, allegedly spoken as he
mounted his horse for the first leg of his return trip
home: "Boys, be ambitious." This probably should
be translated, "Aspire to great things," without the
narrower connotation the word ambition has in contemporary America. Clark was certainly a forceful
individualist, but he had a strong social conscience.
Of a number of national historic monuments in Sapporo, several are associated with Clark.

Sapporo is an inland city, built on the alluvial fan
of the Toyohira River at the base of a mountain
range. The present urban core was laid out in 1869
on a grid plan, divided by an east-west green corridor
into an administrative district on the north and an
amusement and shopping district on the south. The
grid has been the basic street system for planned
cities since time immemorial, but the starkly rational
geometry of Sapporo's layout reflects functional city
planning concepts of the nineteenth century. The
streets, much broader than those of older Japanese
cities, are prosaically named and numbered North
First, South First, East First, and West First, North
Second, South Second, and so forth. If the reader
will visualize a folding chessboard with the fold lying
from left to right, the fold will represent the green
corridor, now Odori Park, running east and west,
which in effect is zero street. The Sosei Canal, originally created to transport construction materials,
runs down the center of another zero street in the
north-south direction, forming a second green boulevard. At the intersection of these is a four-hundred-
foot-tall television tower, which is a powerful landmark (144). An observation deck near the top affords
a panoramic view of the city and looks down on
the full length of Odori Park.

One might think that such a mechanical layout

145

would create a dull city, but it does not. Odori Park
is a convivial, fountain-filled, lantern-lit social corridor a mile long, which from the top of the tower
seems to run directly into the mountains on the west
(145). The clear Toyohira River, whose embank-
ments constitute a linear park, runs diagonally across
the southwest quadrant of the city. The main business street, West Fourth, leads north to a large railroad station plaza, surrounded by hotels, restaurants,

146

and shops, with an extensive network of underground shopping arcades and pedestrian concourses. Sapporo was not bombed in the war, and its physical modernity is due entirely to rapid population growth, not wartime destruction as in older cities. When Clark arrived there in 1877, the city's population was less than ten thousand; the population had multiplied ten times to 100,000 when the first national census was taken in 1920. It had again multiplied by ten, to one million in 1970, and it is now over a million and a half, making Sapporo Japan's fifth-largest city. The city's planners are preparing for nearly two million people by the next century.

With exceptions, the middle-rise architecture is undistinguished, but the tapestry of highly colored, decorative, and often fanciful advertising signs, together with the textured transitional subspaces at street level—which I have described as the distinguishing characteristic of other Japanese cities—

in Sapporo is even more exuberant. The original plan for dividing Sapporo into an administrative district north of the Odori promenade and a commercial and entertainment district south of it has been imperfectly followed. The principal government buildings, including the city hall and the Hokkaido Prefectural Government Building, are located in the north. The last-named modern structure stands next to the Old Prefectural Government Building, an Edwardian red brick edifice, the two united by a traditional Japanese garden with pool (146). However, stores, restaurants, and banks are interspersed throughout this section of the city. That is probably fortunate. As Jane Jacobs noted years ago, single-use districts tend to become lifeless areas after working hours, and— at least in the West—are often dangerous on that account.[39]

I had expected Sapporo to be a drab, uncultured frontier town. I was delightfully surprised at the

147

lively and cosmopolitan ambience I found there, especially at night. A few blocks south of the Odori promenade and parallel to it is another wide boulevard. At the intersection of this and West Fourth Street there is a brightly lit clock. The area around this is an entertainment district known as Susukino, which in Japanese means "field of sedge," suggesting where the urban boundaries were not so very long ago. Susukino is the location of the most popular night spots. Here, one finds the intimate sake and sushi bars that the Japanese love and tourists rarely find because each one is unique and personal to a favorite clientele (147). At night the streetscape is a carnival of lights that extends well up West Fourth Street to the station plaza, full of people until late evening.

With such rapid growth during the twentieth century, on such a rational, functional plan in a previously unsettled region, it is inevitable that Sapporo would become surrounded by suburbs with commercial strips and shopping centers. All this seems very American. But it has not had the effect of depressing or destroying the commercial and social focus of the city center, as suburban sprawl has in the United States. The continued vitality of the urban core may be partly the result of the penchant of working Japanese for after-hours socializing in company groups, and that is hard on gregarious housewives who are isolated in the suburbs. But the official pronouncements of city authorities suggest that the public wants to maintain a cosmopolitan environment and is willing to work hard for it. A Citizens' Charter, adopted in 1963, expresses an urban ideal that consciously includes distemic dimensions along with Japanese proxemic qualities:

We, the citizens of Sapporo, where the chimes of the Clock Tower can be heard, declare:

We shall work hard and build a prosperous city.

We shall keep our skies, streets, grass, and waters clean.

We shall obey laws and make our city a pleasant place for all.

We shall make our city a happy place for our children who will build the future.

We shall raise our cultural standard through cultural exchange with the people of the world.[40]

As regards the last point, Sapporo has established sister-city relationships with Portland, Oregon;

Munich, West Germany; and Shenyang, China. At this writing, the Hokkaido Prefecture is in the process of establishing a sister-state relationship with Massachusetts. The Clock Tower referred to in the Citizens' Charter is on a Victorian wooden building designed by Clark's American assistant and former student William Wheeler, who accompanied him to Sapporo in 1876 and stayed on at the Agricultural College after Clark's departure. The building itself is called the Clock Tower. It served as a drill hall and ceremony hall for the college until the campus was moved to an area north of the railroad station. This nostalgic old structure with its living bell has been preserved as a historical museum and now sits, delightfully rustic behind trees, in the midst of modern buildings on North First Street, opposite the massive new city hall. It is a favorite Sapporo landmark. The present university campus, green and placid in its agricultural setting, is a mere ten-minute walk from the city center. The officially designated historic monument there is a beautiful barn designed by Clark himself with various laborsaving and agriculture-enhancing devices (148). Students come freely into town to socialize in the Susukino entertainment district, where they will find William

148

149

S. Clark's pervasive persona greeting them in a café named Boys Be (149). The university remains nicely integrated into the life of the city; even in the dark hours of the late evening there is no fear of crime.

I have already commented on the celebrated safety of Japanese cities. Physical safety, of both persons and property, is essential for a healthy distemic environment. In stable proxemic local communities, where behavior tends to be controlled by social pressure and people are highly observant of strangers in their midst, policing is often facilitated by citizen surveillance. In distemic spaces, where cultural diversity is the prime objective, any sort of behavioral control based entirely on local norms risks having one group impose its customs and life-style on another, so the protection of persons and the physical environment itself must be achieved through relatively abstract laws that are impartially enforced. Ordinarily these laws are much simpler than the complex and often unconscious codes of traditional cultures. They should be concerned with preventing one individual from interfering with another's free use of the space, limited in the main to essential

traffic rules and to laws for preventing such crimes as murder, robbery, rape, and vandalism. However, laws of this sort are most effectively enforced if supported by one or more proxemic communities that assume responsibility for the public landscape and that, as I have noted, provide interest, vitality, and personality to distemic places by surrounding and interpenetrating them. This is just what happens, it seems to me, in Sapporo, and it shows that the process can occur in a twentieth-century, technologically advanced, planned community. From the point of view of the basic theme of this book, Sapporo is the clearest illustration I have seen in Japan. Its grid plan and distinctive landmarks meet the prime requirement of distemic spaces—that they be legible and accessible to strangers, as well as safe. And yet, the urban fabric is laced with places that meet the basic characteristic of proxemic spaces—territorial enclosure—places that the stranger is likely to find only if escorted there by hospitable local residents, as I was privileged to be. And of course the culture of the latter provides the pervasive quality of the whole scene.

Tsukuba Science City

Sapporo citizens stress their intellectually pioneering spirit, especially in developing up-to-date agriculture. A bank window in the city center displays a large tomato and a green pepper, each with a computer circuit inside. Kobe city officials and their many publications stress their inventiveness in the construction of their new public places. They are proud of the way they moved a hundred million cubic yards of gravel from the mountains to the sea on overhead and underground conveyor belts so as to avoid the noise, commotion, and congestion of truck traffic. It has often been charged that the Japanese are skilled borrowers but do not come up with original ideas. Some of this may simply be Western chauvinism, because the Japanese work in different ways. It also depends on what one means by originality. The Japanese themselves, however, seem to feel they are behind the West in this respect and have built a whole city to deal with the matter. Japanese officialdom, to catch up with the West in basic research, has imported Western rationalism wholesale into a place where

150

the particularity that makes Japan work seems to me to have been eliminated.

Tsukuba Science City was designed to bring together in one planned community the best brains in corporate business and universities. The problem is that it brings together technically polished brains and little else. It was begun twenty years ago in rice paddies and other farmland forty miles north of Tokyo, laid out in the Cartesian rectangles associated with so much city planning around the world. We have seen a particularly beautiful grid city in the case of Kyoto and an effective and humane one in Sapporo. However, the soulless spaciousness of Tsukuba's plan reminded me of Milton Keynes's new city in England, and it lacks even that green desert's more human neighborhoods. One resident I talked to liked the orderly space, and another appreciated the living accommodations, larger than can be had in Tokyo, but many apparently are not happy with this environment. Tsukuba is known for its high suicide rate. Lewis Simons quotes one scientist as saying, "I feel spiritually disjointed here. Despite the space, the green lawns, the clean air—or maybe because of them—I just don't feel at home here the way I did in Tokyo. It's hard to explain to a foreigner, but any Japanese understands—we like to be close together."[41]

Looking at it from the top of one of the inert brick research labs (150), this foreigner did understand. I would as soon live in the Sahara. I saw few people walking the wide streets. There is little human or environmental diversity visible, and one questions whether intellectual diversity can be stimulated in such a place. By contrast, Sapporo, despite its twentieth-century rationality, is socially intimate in a very Japanese way. Likewise, on Kobe's dense Port Island it is unlikely that many of those twenty thousand people living in cliffs of concrete would feel as does the scientist quoted above. The interspaces below and the dramatic harbor surrounding Port Island's sterile International-style towers are teeming with visible activity. Downtown Kobe, with its small, crowded cafés and restaurants, melding mind and spirit with sake, is four miles, not forty miles, away.

In the hope of drawing more people and international attention to Tsukuba, Science Expo '85 was staged with all the architectural clichés that have come to be associated with world's fairs. Upon entering that wonderland, one would think Buckminster Fuller was a promising young inventor! (151). A Japanese architect friend called it a computerized toyland. The children loved it, and it is always a pleasure to see Japanese children in action (152). The lines were so long that there was a three- or four-hour

151

152

wait at the pavilions of corporate giants like Mitsubishi, TDK, and IBM. But the Japanese Government History Pavilion, which I thought was beautifully done in the best Japanese tradition, with artistic life-size reconstructions of the evolution of technology in Japan: mining, hydraulic power, and transportation, was almost empty of visitors. What I saw of the Expo '85 exhibits left me with the feeling that there was a good deal more genuine future to be seen in the neon-lit landscapes of Tokyo's Ginza or Shinjuku and Kobe's Port Island.

The focus of officially sponsored innovation at Expo '85 and its parent Science City is on robotics. Robots are supposed to be the ushers of the next brave new world. But one wonders: obviously robots will be able to do many useful things that humans cannot or do not want to do. Nevertheless, in a world where unemployment could be the greatest menace to civilization, after the threat of nuclear war and overpopulation, should replacing men with machines have top priority in the use of Japan's highest inventive talents? In any case, a streetscape of robots would seem to be a dubious utopia. What a pity if Japan, with its very human, organic specialness, should get too caught up in the short-term competition to lead the world in robotics. There are many people, in and out of Japan, who think

the country has become overly preoccupied with the international race for technological supremacy at the expense of other considerations. If all of Japan were like Tsukuba, one could believe them.

As for technical innovation, I believe that the most beneficent social environment for it is the community of strangers in cosmopolitan cities. People whose innovations tend to rock the village boat escape to the psychologically open, distemic spaces of such centers. Among all those strangers they are more likely to find others with insights into the possibilities for change. The community of strangers is also a community of individuals; in it people must rely on their personal abilities to use universally recognized human signals to communicate who they are—rather than the restrictive codes of a local culture. What matters is the diversity that allows for recombinations. A place like Tsukuba, apparently modeled on the intellectual hothouse communities of high-tech America, would tend to foster a synthetic proxemics based on a rather narrow range of interests and skills.

Traditional societies are usually conservative. They find security in the familiar and try to keep their environment as they have always known it, often behaving as if it had remained unchanged long after it has in fact been altered.[42] Contemporary proxemic cultures based on a fixed set of objectives, like religious cults, also tend to become rigid even if they were initially innovative. The Japanese have a great advantage as a traditional society in that one of their most basic traditions *is* adaptation to change. They were least adaptable during the two Tokugawa centuries and during some ten or fifteen years of this century when they reinstituted that rigid military despotism and tried to force it onto the rest of the world. But throughout most of their history they have been avid learners, first from the Chinese and the Koreans and then from the West. I think that they are able to do this precisely because they territorialize their emotional lives so effectively that they can keep their abstract thought processes free to float in and out of any situation. In the West, by contrast, we tend to invest our rational concepts of life with emotional attachments to the abstract thought systems themselves.

It may well be that the private initial phase of invention is retarded in a group-oriented society like that of Japan. Innovation is inherently dis-harmonizing. The inventor by nature is capable of seeing relationships that are not perceived by those around him. He will at best confuse his colleagues and at worst threaten their security. More than one important invention has been identified by the name of the inventor followed by the word "folly," as in Fulton's Folly for the steamboat. It is understandable that the urge for group harmony would work against radical innovation. And yet, Japan's technical revolution has been led by strong, inventive in-dividualists, such as Soichiro Honda of Honda and Akio Morito, the founder of SONY. Ian Baruma notes: "The interesting thing about such creative oddballs is that once they make it to the top, they almost invariably become traditional masters, laying down the rules for the young to follow. They are more than teachers of technical skills or business methods, in the manner of such figures as Lee Iacocca. In fact they conform more closely to the image of the Confucian sage."[43]

The society that emphasizes the individual also emphasizes the *attribute*, described by Chie Nakane, rather than the *situation*. In the West, and particularly in America, personal achievement gives one status, rewards, and security in the larger society. Thus, the innovator is available for hire to any organization that can offer the highest compensation and the greatest personal advantage. Loyalty to the group is low in the West compared with Japan. The personal security of the individual therefore becomes highly dependent on the essentially abstract attributes of a trade or profession, which can be readily reintroduced into any promising social context. A skill becomes a conceptual territory that is defended by its owner. But I have postulated that it is the older animal core of the human brain that seeks territory, whereas the uniquely human outer cortex with its capacity for abstract ideas requires fluidity and freedom of experience and knows no boundaries. A paradox thus emerges on the Western side of the world: what is most inappropriate to territorialize, the abstract idea, becomes the chief symbol of territorial possession. This is found everywhere in the West, in all the professions, among lawyers, doctors, and architects, in the trade unions, in religions, and most perniciously in the so-called disciplines of academia, which, in the name of academic freedom, are dedicated to erecting walls around units of human thought.

Typical Japanese apparently do not need to do this. Their emotional life is bound up, not in the professions or trades, but in the groups in which they practice them. Since status, income, and a sense of personal worth are related to membership in the group, each individual member can play freely with any idea, so long as it does not negatively affect group harmony. Competition in the West is commonly between individuals who see corporate activities as stepping stones to personal advancement. In Japan, competition is between groups. The competition is no less fierce, but it has different implications regarding ideas. Any idea that can find group consensus will be promoted effectively within that company or agency because its success will be seen as benefiting all members. Tribal territorial impulses are directed largely inward toward main-tenance of a flesh and blood tribe—the com-pany or the agency that has become an *ie*. Ab-stract concepts and logical thought systems, then, can be the subjects of detached *intellectual* attention because they are not emotionally threatening; they will not be implemented without the agreement of the group. In such a situation, there is no reason not to consider any new idea.

In my dealings with Japanese academics, I sense

far fewer disciplinary barriers than we find in American and European universities. However, I find far less awareness of what individuals in other universities in Japan are doing within a particular field of study. One consequence is that the Japanese pursue discussion of an idea with a relaxed curiosity and cheerful detachment that Western institutions profess, but rarely practice. Another consequence may be that an interdisciplinary synthesis of ideas, which is at the core of the most creative thought, is harder to achieve in Western institutions, whereas among individuals in the West such synthesis may be facilitated because they move more readily from one institution to another.

Corporate and Bureaucratic "Innocence"

My own design career began with stage design rather than architecture. Although I soon moved professionally from the theater to the "real world," finding the latter essentially more dramatic, I have continued to think of the environment primarily as a setting for activity rather than as a matter of abstract form, as so many architects and other environmental designers think of it. For many reasons, the landscape of Japan favors an activity-oriented viewpoint. This is true, paradoxically, even in places designed solely for contemplation, such as temple gardens, which will be considered in chapter 5. Before leaving the subject of urban public spaces, a comment on Japanese public theater is in order.

Despite the immense changes of the modernizations of more than a century, the Japanese continue to express a free energy and sensuous vitality in neighborhood and regional festivals in honor of a variety of native gods and spirits. The Gion Matsuri described by my mother is still held every summer in Kyoto. I have not been able to see that myself, but I have watched an equally famous celebration of northern Honshu, the Hirosaki Neputa Festival. There are actually two simultaneous Neputa festivals held during the first week in August in the neighbor cities of Hirosaki and Aomori, invoking legends of a thousand-year-old feudal war. The Neputa were dummies representing men, animals, and birds used to mislead the enemy. The festival in Hirosaki, it is said, symbolizes the departure of the warriors for

the front, and the one in Aomori their triumphant return.

In Hirosaki the townspeople gather in the city center around several blocks of parked floats just before sunset. The participants, who seem to represent half the population, are men, women, and children of all ages, dressed in colorful traditional costumes (153). They organize themselves in various ways, some having picnics on mats beside their vans, imbibing beer or sake. The floats, sixty in all, have been weeks in preparation. They are mostly fan-shaped structures of translucent plastic on steel scaffolds, some twenty-five feet tall, illuminated with electric bulbs powered by portable generators. Typically they are painted with the ferocious faces of two or three ancient samurai and usually one woman, and below them on the rear of the float are mounted a row of large drums. However, some floats are effigies of dragons and animals. There is even a large translucent bulldozer. All are mounted on rubber-tired wheels and are pulled by teams of people.

As the western sky matches their colors in the sunset, the generators start up and the lights on the floats come on one by one. The half of the population not engaged in the parades has been patiently lined up on the sidewalks or in office windows for some time, and since some of them are in costume, it is hard to tell the actors from the audience. In the gathering dusk, with neon lights from stores flashing in the background, the floats move down the street around the central square to the insistent, measured beat of the drums and the rhythmic quaver of flute music (154). The drummers are stripped to the waist, some mounted on top of the drums, others marching behind them, all beating with controlled, muscular vigor (155). The large teams of people in various costumes pull the floats with the joyful ragging motion my mother described at the Gion festival in Kyoto. Periodically they pause in their forward procession to swivel completely around, maintaining the rhythm. The floats are so tall that riders mounted atop them have to fold back the hinged upper portions to clear the overhead utility wires. They do this at the command of a marshall out front with a whistle, without halting the forward motion and without missing a beat. Clearing the wires in this way serves to integrate the ancient festival into the modern technical environment, as does

153

154

155

the steady drone of the gasoline-powered generators on each float, which seems part of the music rather than in conflict with it. The parade continues without letting up for more than three hours, the floats passing at the rate of about one for every three minutes. Then, as the spectators walk home through the dark streets, portions of the parade reappear in various places, and the drums and the flutes can be heard in the distance. The foreign visitor will be a cold person indeed who is not caught up in the spirit of it all.

One of Sapporo's big events is the annual Snow Festival, held each February, when local citizens and visitors from all over the world construct large, exquisitely crafted snow sculptures. This festival began in 1950 when several high school students, to boost their spirits during the long cold winter, built six small snow sculptures in a corner of a city park. That quickly became a tradition, evolving into an international event that now draws an estimated two million visitors from such climatically diverse regions as Korea, China, Australia, the Philippines, Sweden, and America. The five-day festival, which includes performances by Japanese entertainers, first drew

worldwide attention during the Olympic Winter Games in 1972. Here again, we have a proxemic activity in a proxemic space turning into a distemic one without losing its local character. Sapporo also has a lilac festival in the spring; a summer festival in July, when Odori Park is festooned with lanterns and the grounds filled up with beer gardens; and a fall festival.

Remarkably, the Japanese are able to present dramatizations of their traditional myths and legends even to an audience composed entirely of strangers at corporate- or government-sponsored events. On a professional tour of a number of cities in 1985, several hundred landscape architects from all over the world were welcomed by mayors and bureaucrats at lavish receptions. I was amazed at the skill and intensity with which the local flavor of traditional performances was transferred to posh hotels. As noted, a Noh play was presented in the courtyard of the ultramodern Portopia Hotel in Kobe. It was extremely effective in that large square surrounded by rectangular galleries, which were filled with foreigners. Indeed, I found the Noh even more

156

157

158

159

theatrical in that setting than in the intimate traditional theaters for which it was designed.

In Hiroshima, city officials, after many speeches and a sumptuous spread of food and drink, presented the Kagura, the Shinto music and dance of the Chugoku Highlands (156). (Imagine the mayor of Chicago putting on a play about Sleeping Beauty in a Michigan Avenue hotel in such a manner as to give goose pimples to assorted members of an international professional society!) The story concerns a prince who enters a village where the population has been decimated by a monster with eight heads and eight tails. A Japanese Saint George, Prince Susano, enters to the accompaniment of spine-tingling drums and finds a sad local couple whose last surviving daughter, the youngest of six, is about to be eaten by the monster that very evening. He makes a deal with the father: if he slays the dragon, he will take the daughter for his bride.

Susano asks the old man to leave a barrel of sake beside the girl. The monster mistakes the girl's reflection in the sake for the girl herself, drinks the sake with pleasure and predictably gets drunk. This enables the prince to slay him, but not without a truly titanic struggle. Hundreds of yards of brilliantly colored paper, which at times arch twenty feet above the stage floor, coil ferociously around Susano, and hideous clouds of smoke belch forth, all to a mounting crescendo of percussion instruments. For a long while the smoke and coiling paper completely obscure and apparently swallow the prince, but the action shows us that he is still a force to be reckoned with (157–158). Eventually the hero slays the inebriated dragon by cutting off its tails (159). Out of one tail comes a sword, named for the native habitat of the monster, the "Sword of Dark Clouds." It is then dedicated to the "Great God of the Sun."[44]

Thus we have a local rendition of a worldwide environmental dichotomy. But no words or photographs can convey the primitive physical excitement of the performance, an excitement magically transferred to an international audience—strangers to the culture of the local community that generates it. The excitement of this allegorical drama of human existence is briefly shared by a community of strangers gathered in a particular public place. The proxemic and distemic polarities are thus united in a time-space work of art.

5 • Green Space

One often hears that the Japanese respect nature. But one also often hears that they are ruining their beautiful country with their industrial and commercial activities. The traveler in Japan can see evidence either way, depending on what he or she expects to see and wants to find.

At an international conference in Kobe, I heard a prominent British landscape architect describe with high outrage what he saw on the bullet train from Tokyo—three hundred miles of ugly industrial and commercial sprawl and congestion. I have already described some of what I saw on the same train route. There were indeed huge industrial plants belching contaminants into the air (10), and most of the landscape was built up in a congested way. But I also saw—amid the factory towers and storage yards—many temples and gardens, graceful tile-roofed houses in fenced green yards, tranquil rice terraces, fields of tea, playgrounds and parks. The placid canals were undoubtedly polluted, but they often reflected peaceful human activities against a soft sky, somehow mysteriously mated with the mist-shrouded mountains. Was that mist merely smog? Perhaps, but the picture was qualitatively different from Gary or Denver, Birmingham or Manchester. Both human life and natural life seemed much more integrated into it all.

To the contemporary Westerner, "nature" usually means that which is living but not human. To well-off urban Americans in particular, nature in its most perfect form is wilderness. Japan has a great deal of real wilderness. Three-quarters of the land is sparsely inhabited mountains, subject to volcanic eruptions and avalanches, battered by typhoons. The Japanese accept and respect nature's often violent instability as well as its beauty, doing the best they can to minimize the one and tune into the other. But they hardly see in nature a paradise. The Japanese ideal is of nature understood, respected, honored, and obeyed, but shaped by human thought and action, harmonizing man with other living things and even nonliving things. If their built-up landscapes do not follow their ideals any more than ours do, then that is the nature of ideals.

The modern Western image of nature was enduringly expressed in Jean-Jacques Rousseau's concept of the "noble savage." Until his time, the Eden of human origins and the Heaven of human hopes were symbolized by the garden. In the Persian paradise garden, plants were made to bloom in a walled space within an arid landscape through hydraulics devised by man.[1] Primitive hunter-gatherers knew and respected the wilderness, as both forest and desert, but could not afford to ignore its cruel and dangerous aspects. Settled agricultural peoples more often looked to human society in towns and cities for protection and comfort, and the wild hinterland beyond a fringe of cultivated fields was generally considered ugly and threatening.[2]

Rousseau's ideas fostered the romantic landscape fashion in Europe, which was really an idealization not of wilderness but of England's pastoral countryside. It sentimentalized the noble peasant rather than the noble savage. The romantic landscape garden in the eighteenth century remained the province of landed aristocrats, as had the baroque garden before it, and whole villages of real peasants were destroyed or brutally relocated to achieve the desired scenic effects. Rousseau was buried in the middle of a lake on one such estate at Ermonenville, near Paris. However, Rousseau's social ideas influenced egalitarian political movements, and the romantic landscape of England similarly became the model for public parks, designed to return nature to the hard urban spaces of maturing industrial countries. In the mid-nineteenth century, the American Frederick Law Olmsted developed the public park movement into a fine art, as well as a science, starting with New York's Central Park.[3] In so doing, he founded the profession of landscape architecture as it is now practiced in many countries, including Japan. However, until recently, the grounds of temples and shrines served the public as green open space in Japanese cities. Parks as we think of them today were rare in prewar Japan.

The Japanese, to my knowledge, have at no point looked upon human life as divorced from nature. The separation of body from spirit, of mind from matter, characteristic of Judeo-Christian-Muslim thought, is not characteristic of Asian thought. In the biblical story of Genesis, a famous pair of noble savages were banished from God's paradise garden for succumbing to the temptations of nature and asking too many questions. (It is interesting to speculate that the "apple of knowledge" refers to logical thought, and the metaphor of the story suggests the conflict between feeling and reason in our divided brains.) After banishment from the garden, reunion with divine truth lay in an unearthly future. By contrast, the Japanese garden, a favorite habitat for divinity, is the garden of the here and now, which the *kami* shares with man, a place where human thought and actions merge with nature through careful rearrangements of space. Influenced by their native Shinto religions, with their diverse deities, and by Buddhism, with its philosophy of harmony and unity, the Japanese have historically sought to express the spirits of nature through the works of human hands, minds, and machines. Today, there are even temples where a new automobile is brought to be blessed by the local Shinto god (160).

160

The numinous, public green spaces of Japan, and the private garden spaces described in chapter 2, can be traced back to the original wilderness home of mankind more readily than the romantic landscapes can. Makoto Nakamura of Kyoto University's Laboratory of Landscape Architecture relates the traditional Japanese garden to the Japanese penchant for miniaturization, which he says reduces the intermediary elements between man and the natural object, thus intensifying their spiritual relationship. Nakamura notes that the word *niwa*, which the modern Japanese most commonly use for "garden," originally meant a territory for living or a fishing territory in the sea. When Japan's early hunter-gatherer tribes turned to agriculture, part of this living territory became fenced in and was called *sono*, the word for garden in the agricultural sense. Niwa lost its socioeconomic meaning with the emergence of exten-

sive rice agriculture and then became miniaturized into the present aesthetic garden. Nakamura says that niwa "continued to echo its original form by reflecting the totality of the environment . . . thus appealing to all of man's senses."[4]

In the twentieth century, Japan has been concerned mainly with modernizing its economy and, following the devastation of World War II, with rebuilding its industry. It did not emulate the extensive urban park programs that developed in Europe and the Americas. The home-in-a-garden in the private domain (for those fortunate to still have such homes in the immediate postwar period) and the temple-in-a-garden in the public domain served a hardworking population as restorative green space. As industrial expansion gave way to a period of economic stability, and then slowdown during the oil crises of the 1970s, concern with both the quality of life and the quality of the environment emerged in Japan as in other developed nations. An affluent and rapidly growing urban population, increasingly confined to apartment buildings without home gardens, sought organized recreation and contact with nature. This required larger and more active spaces than those offered by the miniaturized contemplative environments surrounding shrines, temples, villas, and castles. In the last two decades, Japan has started to "catch up with the West" in the matter of public parks, both urban and regional, with the same dedication and energy it had devoted to catching up on the industrial and commercial scene. Ironically, their park and conservation programs are expanding, while those in the United States are declining.

I think of the publicly accessible open spaces called parks—which involve artfully arranged natural elements: plants; landform; water; and wild animals—as the most benign and joyful of distemic spaces. Indeed, I was led to invent the word distemic, to be used in place of cosmopolitan, largely to describe the human activities and psychological conditions provided by parks. The word cosmopolitan does not quite fit these rural or wild places. City parks usually intensify the awareness of nonhuman nature by their juxtaposition to manmade structures in urban surroundings. Even the state and national parks, intended to preserve wildlife unchanged by man, are essentially human and sociable places because of their planned accessibility.

Human beings congregate in parks for no other purpose than the pleasure of being there, in settings that transcend local culture and tribal conventions. This can happen because we are, after all, members of a single species of animal, biologically adapted to, and therefore presumably attracted by, natural elements and other living beings. Different cultures and even different social groups within cultures respond to, use, and expect different aspects of nature, but there is a common dimension in green spaces not found in manmade urban environments.

Environmental planning in Japan does have a long history. One of the early acts of the Meiji government in 1875 was to proclaim that each prefecture must preserve places of scenic beauty, designating them for the use of the people. In 1920, the City Planning Law authorized not only park planning, but also the designation of "landscape districts." After the 1923 earthquake that leveled Tokyo and Yokohama, restoration plans included a few large parks and many small ones. At that time, regional greenbelts for Japanese cities, influenced by European planning concepts such as the classic Greater London Plan, were proposed. This would have provided public parks and conserved farmlands and woodlands. Preparations for World War II, however, prevented the materialization of those plans. By 1937, Air Defense Parks became part of the city landscape, intended more for civil defense observation and firebreaks than recreation. However, large-scale green open spaces were planned in 1940 to commemorate the supposed 2,600th anniversary of the Japanese empire. Land was purchased by the government for that purpose in twenty-six cities by the end of 1941, when Japan's war with China became World War II.

In 1945, the Special City Planning Law was enacted for the restoration of 120 cities destroyed in the war, which had left an estimated ten million people homeless. This law included the designation of greenbelts, but economic and industrial priorities nullified its effect. Nevertheless, by 1956 the City Park Law paved the way for the current "greening" policies, which began in 1962 with the Law Concerning the Preservation of Trees for the Maintenance of the City's Beauty and Landscape. The Ministry of Construction began a policy of building parks in municipal riverbeds in 1965. This was followed by the Historical Landscape Conservation Law in 1966. It was in that year that the new town of Tama described in chapter 2 (50–53) was planned on the basis of the "natural topographic scheme."[5]

In 1968, the cabinet of the national government celebrated the centennial anniversary of the Meiji Restoration by constructing Memorial Park in the Saitama Prefecture, the first of a system of twelve parks planned as *city parks*, to be sponsored by the government and called National Government Parks. These were launched under a different program with a name confusingly similar to natural preservation areas called National Parks. Seven of the National Government Parks near big cities are now open to the public. Prior to 1968, the only parks administered under the direct supervision of the government had been the Imperial Palaces in Kyoto and Tokyo and the former Imperial Garden at Shinjuku. Presently, in addition to the city-oriented National Government Parks, there are twenty-seven wilderness parks called National Parks. These large regional reservations are set up on the British model and are not wholly owned by the government, as are their American counterparts, but are broadly protected areas allowing private farming and other activities. There are also fifty-four quasi-national parks and three hundred prefectural parks. A series of five-year environmental protection programs, begun in 1972, has accompanied development of these local parks, along with much greening of city streets and neighborhoods.[6] This has complemented a significant amount of pollution abatement and environmental quality legislation and action.[7]

Tokyo Green Spaces

Tokyo's Hibiya Park, reportedly the first municipal park in Japan, was planned back in 1887, but it met with opposition and was not completed until 1903. It is perhaps the most Western of parks in Tokyo, large parts of it laid out in a symmetrical, rectangular pattern of walks, flower beds, pools, and sculptures (161), all focused on a round central fountain (162). The tall buildings of the modern central city form a wall on two sides, intensifying the restful feeling of immersion in plant life and in the most genial kind of human life, as

161 162

163 164

does Olmsted's Central Park in New York. But here, the art of all they do applied to both design and maintenance, coupled with the lack of street crime, fills the American visitor with shame for the shabbiness of so many parks at home, including parts of Central Park. The Imperial Hotels have all faced Hibiya Park (163), as some of New York's most prestigious hotels face Central Park. The hotels and looming office buildings are a powerful contribution to the distemic presence in such public spaces.

The nearby Imperial Palace, secluded behind its gates and guardhouses (164), insures a proxemic Japanese ambience. The Imperial Palace Outer Garden, lying between moats, was designated as a public park in 1947 and is now a dramatic transition zone between the palace grounds and the central city (7, 96, 165). Because such parks are distemic,

165

the use of them does not really vary that much between cultures. Apart from sports like tennis, the basic activities are walking and sitting, which combine nature watching with people watching as they do anywhere. In Japanese parks, as on the streets, the stranger does not *feel* observed because the Japanese avoid unnecessary interaction through casual eye contact. But one is probably observed without knowing it, and if a reason presents itself to connect with a stranger, the response is likely to be remarkably open and warm, and often very helpful. If an American looks lost, fingering a map, he will probably soon find an English-speaking Japanese at his elbow, politely asking if directions are needed.

The tendency of the Japanese to move in groups is very evident in the major parks. On the immaculate green lawns of the Imperial Palace Outer Garden, under carefully pruned trees with the tall towers of Maranouchi looming behind them, groups of dark-suited businessmen sit in circles on sunny weekdays, eating lunch or just chatting. Often two or three youngsters will detach themselves from the platoons of uniformed school children that seem to be everywhere in the public spaces of Japan, asking the foreigner where he is from, telling him where they are from, wanting him to pose for a snapshot with them. The uniforms do not make these young people seem regimented; they express rather than suppress their individual personalities.

The relaxed energy and activity of these genial, accessible public spaces is in marked contrast to the sense of silent tranquillity within the inner moat and walls of the Imperial Palace grounds. These are open to the public at certain hours, but only by appointment. The seclusion of the emperor and his family in all that high-priced urban land is accepted as natural by the Japanese, not considered elitist isolation as it certainly would be in America. The remoteness of the emperor from daily life is precisely what makes him an important national symbol, as expressed in the Japanese Constitution, and this symbol remains strong nearly half a century after he disclaimed his divinity under pressure of the American occupation. That divinity has traditionally been symbolic, not an expression of personal megalomania. The present emperor is reported to be a gentle, modest man, and some of his predecessors were so modest as to be ineffectual as practical rulers. But the

emperors remained a symbol of the nation even when the real power was in the hands of the shoguns. The emperor's role at the apex of the Japanese hierarchical concept of life, in which rank matters so much and what is not visible but still palpable is as important as what is clearly in view, is well expressed spatially in the palace grounds in Tokyo. Although the palace is hidden from most vantage points, everyone knows that it is there.

According to Seidensticker, the Meiji government allocated five public parks as early as 1873, preceding the plans for Hibiya Park, but only one of the five parks, Ueno, has remained a green open space.[8] Ueno Park, located on a ridge of land above what is now the huge Ueno Station, was originally the site of two Tokugawa-era funeral temples. It was also the place where the Edo shogun made his last stand in Tokyo in resistance to the new government that followed the Meiji Restoration. Ueno, one of Tokyo's major subcenters, is on the northern edge of the central city at the border between the High City and the Low City. The park lies above the large railroad station, which appears to be built into the hill (166). From the main hall of the terminal, one actually climbs to the train platforms above. The street that bounds the eastern edge of Ueno Park looks across the intense commercial node around the station (167). Thus, the railroad hub not only provides citywide access to the park, but also a kinetic urban setting for its serene and shady recesses.

One of the focal points of Ueno Park is the National Museum of Western Art. Haru Matsukata Reischauer describes the dramatic origins of the initial collection for this museum, which was acquired by her uncle Kojiro Matsukata for his country at his own considerable expense while he was in Europe between the wars. His efforts to bring the collection home were frustrated by the growing international hostilities and diplomatic red tape, and he never lived to see it properly displayed. The museum in Ueno Park is the result of efforts by his friends, both Japanese and Western, after his death. It was designed by Le Corbusier, and it opened in 1959.[9]

The planted walkways, grassy malls, and graveled plazas in the vicinity of the museum are punctuated with sculptures by Occidental modernists, art works that look at least as at home there as in their place of origin (168). Great art is, after all, essentially dis-

166

167

168

temic—it inexplicably touches on the universal in human experience, even while expressing the private personality and proxemic culture of the artist. In my view, sculpture is as natural and necessary in an urban park as are trees and shrubs. On the northern end of Ueno Park, across a wide mall, near the Tokyo University of Fine Arts, is the National Museum. To the west of a long mall is the Tokyo Metropolitan Art Museum. There is a zoological garden, roamed over by hordes of school children in uniform—eager, exuberant, disciplined, as naturally charming as the animals they come to see and considerably freer despite their organized groups (169).

Ueno Park is a place for the solitary stroller to pause and examine the lush and varied flora. There are several numinous spaces that are uniquely Japanese (170, 171), including more than one shrine (172), and on the eastern edge a cemetery. The cemetery appears to be a miniaturized high-rise necropolis blending quite marvelously with the neo-Bauhaus skyline beyond (173). On the western side of the ridge on which the park sits, an elevated walkway connects with the top of a park building below, and a stone staircase leads down to the edge of Shinobazu Pond, spangled with lotus leaves and populated by water birds (174).

169 171

170

172

173

174

A short distance to the east of Ueno, near the Sumida River, which is unfortunately no longer visible from the park, is another sociable center, Asakusa, site of the large Kannon Temple. This also was one of the five park areas planned by the Meiji government, but it did not remain an open green area. All through the Meiji and Taisho periods, right down to Pearl Harbor, it was a center for theaters, music halls, movie palaces, and other commercial amusement enterprises. Seidensticker reports that in 1903 Asakusa had the first movie theater in Japan.

He describes Asakusa up to World War II, when it was leveled in the bombing, as "the great pleasure warren of a pleasure loving city."[10]

Today the precincts of the Kannon Temple consist of a major bazaar with a long mall lined with shops leading to the temple, a Tokyo version of Quincy Market. At the entrance to the bazaar, under a great red torii, there hangs a huge paper lantern (175). Below this lantern, standing by a column of the great torii with the effigy of some deity in a shrine above him, one may find the slender figure of a monk (176, 177). Over the long arcade there is a steel frame containing lights. This frame supports a removable awning. One spring, which was unusually late, I found the arcade decorated with live cherry blossoms flown in from Kyushu and wired to it as if they had grown on its ferric columns. The stalls sell a wide variety of cheap and gaudy goods. On the side streets you can find small ryokan (Japanese-style inns). At

175

176

177

the far end of the arcade, the great roof of the
Kannon Temple looms over an open plaza. People
of all types and sizes mill around the smaller
buildings and stalls where a variety of goods are sold
(178). Clouds of incense drift up from the viscera-
red recesses of the temple. To the left of the main
building is a five-storied pagoda, and behind it a
garden.

There are a number of other public open spaces,
many associated with temples or shrines, but
generally Tokyo does not strike the visitor as a city
of parks. That does not mean that it lacks greenery.
Indeed, it has long been argued that Japan did not
need parks because houses had domestic gardens,
and, as noted, many do, although much of Tokyo
is so densely populated that there is little room for
any but a few potted plants, even in single-family
houses. And there are many cemeteries.

In the downtown area, some buildings have
spacious grounds, as in the upper center of photo
179, and active recreation is provided for in fenced-
off spaces. These are designed for specific games,
as in the caged sports area in the foreground. In
industrial sections there are pockets of trees among
the massive, blocky buildings lining the canals, as
seen in the view from the monorail that connects

180

Tokyo with its Haneda Airport. Many streets have trees (180), and high-rise hotels often loom above masses of green. Shinjuku is surrounded by green areas, including a large park and some smaller parks and gardens (181). The main avenue that passes through Yoyogi Park near Shinjuku is now closed to traffic on Sundays and is filled with bands of youths playing musical instruments or breakdancing (182). There are various types of parks on the suburban outskirts of the city, often in the river

181

182

183

floodplains that cannot be developed, and all are
heavily used by the ubiquitous uniformed children
and others. The youngsters in photo 183 are Boy
Scouts. In back of a vast string of containerized piers
on Tokyo Bay, an elaborate modern park has been
constructed (184). It looks like a suburban town
common in the middle of surprisingly vacant land.
I was told that a town is planned for there. I like
the priority system that builds the park first and the
town second!

184

Parks in Other Cities

Japanese cities, like cities anywhere, vary considerably in personality. The same can be said of parks. As noted, the Flower Road in Kobe, which is really a linear, vehicular park, connects the city center with the harbor. But the most visible green spaces of that city are on the looming Rokko mountain range. These mountains were denuded of trees at the end of the nineteenth century, but a reforestation program was begun in 1903 and they now appear to be covered by a primeval forest. Much of this is parkland, and more is planned. There is a large arboretum and Central Wood Park, started in the 1960s, on one forested mountain above the city (185). In 1982 ambitious plans were developed by Kobe city authorities for a Forest of Kobe. This is focused on a valley between two mountains, which faces the city and still retains its natural beauty. The declared objective of the plan is to reconcile conservation with the great demand for development and for recreational facilities by the expanding, energetic, commercial, cosmopolitan population. The planned area currently contains a number of temples, of which Tenjoji atop Mount Maya is deemed particularly important as symbolic of the port city because it has been a sacred Buddhist place of worship for sailors on the Seto Inland Sea since the seventh century.

The officials planning the Forest of Kobe declare that they wish to honor the history of their city as one formed by the mountains and the sea. They propose to combine ancient Japanese concepts of landscape design with modern environmental engineering, using a model taken from a historic gardening book, *Sakutiki*, written ten centuries ago. Particular attention will be paid to harmonizing views of this valley from central Kobe with the surrounding and more distant mountains. One device will be to create woods of deciduous and flowering trees that will stand out from the prevailing evergreen forest.[11]

Among the present parklands of the Rokko range is an agricultural park on a sand and gravel mesa where the Mediterranean-like climate of the Inland Sea coast produces figs, grapes, pears, and mandarin oranges along with other agricultural products. A "wine castle" produces Kobe wine from the park grapes. There are sheep, cows, rabbits, and other animals. This park is also a base for experiments in urban agriculture. At the western end of the range, where one mountain was shaved to a third of its original height to provide fill for Port Island, a new town called Suma was started in 1961 with a projected population of 113,000 people. This new town not only includes extensive local green space, but in constructing it great care was taken to preserve the skyline as seen from Kobe and to maintain the windbreak that the mountains provide to the city. In the same area there is a large and complex Comprehensive Sports Park with two stadiums and a range of recreational facilities. There is also the Otoshiyama Relics Park, ancient home of the god Otoshi, patron of farmers, laden with shards, remains of houses, and tombs. Nearer the sea, there is a huge mound-tomb called Goshikizuka, dating from the late fourth century, which was reconstructed in 1965 and is designated a National Historic Relic. There are a number of Western-style parks, one quite large and impressive with neoclassic fountains and pavilion, as well as a seaside park and an offshore Ocean Fishing Park. There are two parks on the new Port Island.

In addition to its various park projects, Kobe has an official tree planting program, which began in 1971 and has planted throughout the city a million trees a year for fifteen years. The target is to maintain 70 percent of the city in its present green state and

185

to green 30 percent of the built-up area. As a consequence, the major arterial streets of Kobe, including the area under the monorail to Port Island, are now graced with trees (186). Where the central city backs up against the base of the mountains, traditional streets and shrines are maintained (187). The overall sense for the visitor is of a green, clean, contemporary human habitat firmly embedded between those two basic geomorphic elements, the mountains and the sea. Kobe's modernity, so distinctively fitted to such a grand natural setting, makes that port city seem appropriately welcoming to a stranger.

186

187

Sapporo has no sea; there I felt at home rather than welcomed. I have already described Odori Park, Sapporo's recreational centerpiece. The city has a number of other parks, in addition to the banks of the Toyohiro River, also referred to above. In the administrative northern section, not far from the prefectural government buildings, there are the Botanical Gardens, covering nine city blocks. To the south is Nakajima Park, containing the Nakajima Sports Center, the Winter Sports Museum, a municipal

188

189

pool, and a Japanese garden. On the western mountain, overlooking the city, is a terraced park (188). The day I was there a number of armed police were in evidence: the emperor's son was present on an official visit. But the public was not restricted.

By far the most interesting of Sapporo's parks, to my mind, is its recently opened Art Park. The first phase of this park, which will take fifteen years to complete, is situated about seven miles south of the city center on a forested hillside, with the outlying residential districts in view in the distance (189). It is intended to be a link between the city and its suburbs. The entrance area on the lower flat part is, according to the planners, "allocated to facilities related to the daily lives of visitors." These facilities include craft studios ranged around a pond, which has a floating abstract sculpture that turns gently, like an aquatic mobile. From this, winding granite stairs lead to the Symbolic Sculpture Plaza, where there is another pool fed by a river above. Opposite the plaza, the handsome park center building is set against the hillside. On the hills above is the Sapporo Sculpture Garden, where the work of forty-five contemporary Japanese sculptors—ranging from gleaming abstractions in stainless steel to bronze figurative pieces and dark wooden Ainu totems—is set on grassy slopes, in wooded glens, and along the river ravine (190, 191). I have never seen a more effective synthesis of the arts of sculpture, landscape architecture, building architecture, and town planning.

190

191

Of all the city parks in Japan that I have visited, the most universal in style and symbolism—not the most beautiful, but the most distemic, and also for tragic reasons the most modern—is the Peace Memorial Park in Hiroshima. Here, the common fate of all humanity, if we do not mend our ways, is made manifest in the ultimate war memorial. Peace Park lies in the center of the city whose name is synonymous with nuclear devastation. Like Tokyo, Hiroshima is built on a delta. Its chief landmark, standing across the river from Peace Park, is the ruined dome of what was once the Prefectural Industrial Promotion Hall (this name resounds in irony!). The shell of the hall is the only remaining structure from the ruins of the blast that leveled the city (192, 193). It has much the same effect on the observer as the ruins of Coventry Cathedral, destroyed by Hitler's incendiary bombs and preserved by the British as an antiwar statement.

192

193

194

The park itself lies on an island formed by two of several branches of the river that forms the delta, at the southern end of the park, where the broad tree-shaded Peace Boulevard crosses the island. Facing north toward the dome along a planted mall is the Peace Memorial Museum, designed by the noted architect Kenzo Tange. It became, according to Botond Bognar, "the first world-famous building of Japan's modern era."[12] No doubt the theme and location of the building contributed to its world fame. Inside the long, horizontal, rather noncommittal concrete box on pilotis, exhibits of the first atomic bombing present the visitor with a shattering experience. A large diorama shows the leveled city of Hiroshima ringed by the mountains that contained and intensified the blast, its dead rivers weaving through a demolished landscape. Above hangs a small round ball showing the precise position of the bomb when it exploded, very near the present Peace Park (194). Among the mementos is a watch that stopped at the exact time of the blast, 8:15, in the pocket of a man standing on a bridge nearly a mile away, the watch a gift from a soldier son who had just returned from the war to greet him (195).

Kengo Futagawa's pocket watch.
The blast occurred when he was on the Kannon Bridge (1600 meters from the hypocenter). The time was 8:15 when the pocket watch, which had been presented to him as a gift from his eldest son, Kazuo, stopped. Kazuo was just returning home from the army and was just in front of the house when his father died.

Father's watch never moved again

195

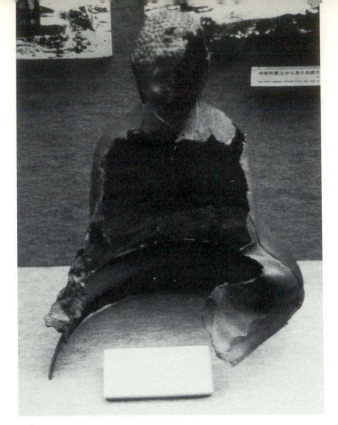

There is the shadow of a person etched into a stone bench against a building where he had been sitting, and there is the eviscerated shell of a bronze Buddha (196). Another diorama shows in three dimensions two women and a child against a background of flames, staggering through the rubble with their skin hanging from extended hands (197). One wishes that the leaders of all the world's nuclear powers could be made to convene in that museum once a year in early August. Yet, as frequently noted by peace activists, few of the world's government leaders have visited it.

196

197

198

199

Outside the museum, a Flame of Peace is scheduled to burn continuously until the day when there will be no more nuclear weapons. The arch of one of the many monuments to that hope frames the skeletal dome of the Industrial Promotion Hall (198). Visitors lay wreaths of flowers at the arch. On another monument to peace, people drape chains of origami cranes. And yet the atmosphere of this park and the city as a whole is a bright contrast to the inside of the museum. The whole environment seems to be ablaze with flowers, light, and life. The groups of school children who flash the Allied "V-for-victory" sign of World War II have no memory of the event (199). These civic, if not actual, descendants of the victims of that holocaust seem to hold no resentment toward visitors from the nation that has the dubious distinction of being the first to drop the Bomb, therewith totally changing the face of their environment. One visitor who was there with me marveled that "a city which had so much death now has so much life." Another friend has commented that this was true when he first visited Hiroshima in 1958, only thirteen years after the bombing.

200

The lobby of the Hiroshima Grand Hotel surrounds an atrium garden (200). The circular building of the Hiroshima Museum of Art, commingling Western and Japanese works, sits in a serenely modern walled enclave. Not far away is the Shukkeien Garden, dating from the early seventeenth century. It retains the form of the ancient stroll garden, including the Chinese bridge (201), but every living thing in it was destroyed forty years ago—except for one large Ginkgo tree (202). That tree has a huge scar on the blast side (203), but it lives! For me, that tree is the most moving monument to hope in all of that memorial scene.

201

202

縮景園（爆心地から約1,350メートル）
Shukkeien Garden (1,350 meters from the Hypocenter)

203

204

Regional Parks

Hiroshima City is surrounded by a variety of parks and recreational green spaces, including a botanical garden and the mountaintop Hijiyama Park, which affords a fine view of the city. Not far away is a famous seaside shrine, which we will turn to later. The shortage of land in Japan's central cities, combined with the mobility offered by automobiles and other modern forms of transportation, has caused parks to be built outside of city centers, often serving more than one city. The aforementioned National Government Park program (not to be confused with the National Parks) is designed to help cities build recreational open spaces of this kind.

Along the northerly shore of Kyushu, across Hakata Bay from the city of Fukuoka, is one of the National Government Parks, the Umi-no Nakamachi Seaside Park. It was started in 1980 on the site of a former U.S. Air Force base after five years of planning. The runways were dug up and the air force buildings removed to provide a large recreational area of white sand, smooth beaches, and activity centers including cycling trails and animal woods. At the main entrance the visitor is greeted by a contemporary pavilion with a large fountain frothing like breakers against a fence of sea waves and gulls. The colonnade of the pavilion frames a distant mountain across the flat pine-clad sands (204). A restaurant sits by a reed-rimmed pond, approached by a zigzag pedestrian causeway (205). Even in this

205

206

postmodern park, essential Japanese design principles of asymmetry and indirection are to be found. The most prominent landmark is a large, multicolored ferris wheel, adjacent to a playground designed to stretch young bodies and young imaginations (206).

Of these regional metropolitan parks, one of the most innovative is the Yodogawa Riverside Park that stretches for twenty-two miles along the Yodo River, flowing from Kyoto to Osaka and connecting several urban subcenters along the way. This is an ecological park, departing from both Japanese and European classical traditions, and it appears to have been designed by natural preservationists rather than

by landscape artists (207). The long, narrow strip covering both banks of the Yodo River is divided into a string of alternating zones of three types. The map of the park with its zones in three colors looks like a necklace of beads on a string. One color of bead represents a nature zone, which is limited to scenic viewing and observation of nature, mostly wetland grasses and bird life. Here, city people confined to hard landscapes can, within a short travel distance from their homes, observe the seasonal changes and other rhythms of nature minimally affected by man. In this type of zone facilities are limited to viewing stations and minor maintenance

207

roads. In the second type, the green grass zone, children and adults can interact more freely with the environment in a natural setting of ponds, streams, and valleys among gently sloping hills covered with wild grasses. Zones of this type are placed so as to act as buffers between the fragile nature zones and the third category, the active recreational zones. In the active recreational zones, sports facilities are provided adjacent to major roads, railways, and built-up areas (208). Because this park is planned as part of a flood control program, structures are limited to a maximum height of one meter so as not to impede the flow of high water. The exceptions are toilets and backstops, which must be removable.

208

209

Since it is a linear park traversing a large metropolitan area, travel time for regional residents is minimized, and many need only walk from their homes (209). The public road that runs along some of the riverbank is intermittently closed to vehicular traffic but open to pedestrians (210). This accessibility has resulted in an 80 to 90 percent use of active sports facilities on weekdays, a high figure for a regional park. On weekends, according to a park department brochure, "the luck of gaining access to fields and courts is one out of ten." After only ten years of use, nearly three million people annually patronize this park. What is especially nice about this thin, long river recreation space is that it seems to be integrated with the surrounding urban and agricultural landscape and with the lives of people who reside along the way. It appears to be one long neighborhood park, despite its scale more proxemic than distemic.

In Hokkaido, a half-hour drive from Sapporo, Napporo Forest Park was dedicated in 1968 as a Prefectural Park to commemorate the centennial of the island's development. The major landmark of this five-thousand-acre suburban park is the Hokkaido Memorial Tower, an attractive shaft of bronze-colored corten steel that can be seen from the city center. The park contains a beautifully designed historical museum and a historic village, but most of its area is natural forest. Indeed, 60 percent of Sap-

210

poro's land area is forested. Ten miles south of Sapporo is a National Government Park called Takino Suzurin Hillside, still under construction along a mountain river with a waterfall (211). Closer to the city is a small park with the larger-than-life bronze statue of William S. Clark pointing over the plain of planted fields, declaring, "Boys, be ambitious" (212), large photos of which greet travelers arriving and leaving at Chitose Airport.

211

212

213

214

Inland Sea National Park

Although Japan is one of the world's two largest producers of automobiles, second only to the United States, it has not yet developed highways as extensive as those in America and parts of Europe. But they are working on it. The Japanese obviously love speed on wheels as much as anyone, and the highway authorities are extending the urban street greening to the highways they have (213, 214). But planes, trains, and buses are the preferred form of transportation for long distances. The Shinkansen (bullet train) now runs from Tokyo to the gateway of Kyushu Island, covering over seven hundred miles in seven hours. As a consequence, the wild National Parks (not to be confused with the city-oriented National Government Parks described above) are not as badly affected by automobiles as such preserved areas are in America and Europe. For example, a rather tortuous two-lane road takes the traveler by bus from Beppu on northern Kyushu through Aso National Park, past the active volcano of Mount Aso, with the world's greatest caldera basin. The bus traveler sees many other buses but relatively few cars. Not all of the preserved areas are wild. High in the mountains there are lavish resort hotels and whole hillsides of clipped azaleas (215–217). In spacious Hokkaido, automobiles are

215

216

217

the main means of transportation for a three-hour drive over a winding two lane road to a wild national park surrounding a large lake (218). By contrast, the trip to Nikko, where the Tokugawa shoguns built a spectacular shrine to their founder high in the mist-shrouded mountains north of Tokyo, takes three to four hours on a four-lane auto freeway, and the traffic jams on Sunday night are like those going into New York at the end of a weekend.

Rural roads, whether traversed by bus or car, offer spectacular scenery, with ample provision for enjoying it. On the ridge above Takamatsu in a parklike setting off the main highway, there is a revolving restaurant from which one gets a slowly shifting panorama of the surrounding mountains, the city, and the sea. Outside the spacious rotating dining room, there are vine-covered terraces looking out over the islands of the Inland Sea (219) and the port of Takamatsu (220). In a discussion of the viewing stations at Takamatsu's famous Ritsurin Park, Richie remarks on the Japanese passion for viewing their scenery: "I cannot imagine any Japanese, even two warriors engaged in a life-and-death struggle, not stopping to admire the view."[13] This is not farfetched. Ancient artwork suggests they may have done just that, and World War II soldiers may have done the same. Much of the emotional impact of Yoshida's *Requiem for Battleship Yamato* (quoted briefly in chapter 3) comes from its vivid description of the world as it looked to those doomed men on that doomed ship, as, despite their certainty of their imminent death, they did take extensive time to contemplate the view from it.[14]

The opportunities offered to Japanese vacationers for viewing along their way are many and carefully arranged, and the foreigner is caught up in the spirit of it. The view of and from the Inland Sea is unforgettable. Because no highways presently connect the three islands surrounding it, a vast number of ferries crisscross this sea, most of which is a great watery park, actually designated as Seto-naikai (Inland Sea) National Park. A significant part of Japan surrounds this island-studded park. The Seto Inland Sea is long and narrow, stretching for two hundred and fifty miles westward from Osaka Bay between Honshu and the island of Shikoku, with the island of Kyushu closing its western end. It is almost a quarter of the length of the main Japanese archipelago, dotted with hundreds of cone-shaped islands, large and small, and sheltered from the strong swells of the Pacific by narrow straits. It is certainly the gentlest sea that I have ever sailed upon.

Along with recreation, it is a center of commercial fishing, shipping, and mundane transportation. As noted, the Japanese national park system is like that of the British, protected and regulated but not owned in fee by the government, as are the United States national parks. Much of the Seto-naikai is far from wild. One wishes it could be protected from any more ports like Osaka, Kobe, and even Takamatsu, dramatic as they are. Some of the shoreland is scarred by mines, and a huge bridge under construction will leapfrog the islands from Okayama on Honshu to Sakaide on Shikoku, just west of Takamatsu. This may have the same unfortunate impact on Shikoku Island as New York's Verazzano Narrows Bridge had on Staten Island twenty-five years ago, forcing explosive urbanization of an environmental oasis.

Nevertheless, it is hard to spoil such scenery as the Inland Sea, and great care is taken with much of it. The ferry terminal at Takamatsu is greened right up to the gangway (221). The terminal building, which in the United States would likely be dreary and dirty and offer hot dogs, cool coffee, and warm beer in plastic containers, if anything, here has a restaurant facing a garden with a fountain. The main deck of the ferry itself has lighted floral displays around its stairways. In the setting sun, from the stern as the ferry pulls away, a tank farm looks like a contemporary sculpture garden. The conical islands drift by on the gentle swells as if they were materializations from a Hiroshige woodcut. The terminal on the Honshu side is not nearly as attractive as the one on Shikoku, but it has a pavilion on a floating dock with a roof that matches the mountains in the background.

221

Agricultural Green Space

Notwithstanding the beauty of the various kinds of parks, the working agricultural landscape of Japan is also worthy of much viewing. So little of this mountainous country is suitable for cultivation that agricultural and urban land are tightly intermeshed in the densely populated lowlands and flat mountain plateaus. It is not unusual to see a pagoda rising above farm fields (222). In the mountain village of Ohara, north of Kyoto, tilled land goes right up to the doorsteps of nonfarm houses (223). Japanese agricultural authorities have been struggling to enact and enforce laws for the preservation of farmland, with questionable success in the laissez-faire land market of rapidly urbanizing areas. But considerable continuity is maintained by heavy government subsidies to rice farmers, most of whom are part-time growers working in the city.

222

223

224

Farmers are able to work their land part-time by using sophisticated agricultural machines such as rice planters. Rice is grown all the way from subtropical Kyushu to northern Hokkaido.

One might wish for the preservation of whole agricultural regions, for the best of Japan's farmscape is immensely beautiful. The glittering geometry of the flooded fields, textured with soft green shoots in even but slightly irregular rows like coarse cloth, edged by intricately interwoven dikes, dams, and canals, creates a strangely splendid sort of land architecture in counterpoint to the mountain landforms and the river channels that supply them (224–226). Despite the demands of hydraulic technology, the rice terraces form patterns of great variety and complexity. In Honshu and in Kyushu, the graceful tile roofs and low profile of traditional farmhouses richly augment the setting: manform and landform in a symbiotic embrace (227). In Hokkaido, where the winter climate is harsh and the snows heavy, there is a different style of house with sharply peaked roofs. Here the land seems more open, and the farmhouses sit alone in the fields, reminiscent of New England in shape and mood, except for the rice agriculture (228). The geometry here is similar to that of the south, but starker, the hydraulics less hidden by lush flora, but with their own constructivist fascination (229). Although modern engineering techniques are used for planting, harvesting, and maintaining water levels, one can still find the footprints of the human cultivator imprinted in the rich muck beneath the shining water (230).

225

226

227

228

229

230

Japan's open space planning, like that of other developed countries, includes the preservation of numerous traditional urban spaces as national historic districts. One of these is an old section of Kurashiki, a port on the Inland Sea dating back to early Tokugawa times. The preserved area owes much to the wealthy Ohara family, cotton merchants who founded the city's spinning industry. These few blocks constitute a spatial work of art, with their graceful white stucco buildings under projecting black tile roofs ranged along a street built on the stone banks of an L-shaped canal overhung with willows (231–233). Beyond the 90-degree bend where a bridge crosses the canal, one finds exquisite examples of the fenced house-with-garden, described in chapter 2, in which the clearly separate, private home domain complements the public domain of street, bridge, and canal (234). Less imposing but equally classic are the small, inviting, highly textured transitional zones of the commercial streetscape nearby (235).

Old Kurashiki has the same sort of appeal to Japanese and foreign tourists seeking nostalgia as do places like old Savannah, Charleston, or Saint Augustine in the United States and countless well pre-

234

235

233

served towns and villages in Europe. It is easy to disparage the self-conscious and somewhat contrived "oldness" of these places, so crowded with modern people who do not live there. It is undoubtedly more thought provoking to consider human nature in out-of-the-way villages like those described somewhat wistfully by Richie in *The Inland Sea*.[15] But the thing to do in places like Kurashiki, where proxemic icons are converted almost entirely into distemic symbols, is to enjoy the clash of time-space images as a kind of public theater, asking only that it be done well. In Kurashiki it is done well. And not all of it pretends to be either old or native. Among the features of Kurashiki is another museum of Western art, founded by the twentieth-century descendants of the Ohara clan. It and an anthropology museum compete somewhat ineffectually for tourist attention with the Rural Toy Museum. But the crowds of strangers and the shops that sell toys to them cannot obscure the genius loci in the numinous spaces of this artfully preserved town.

Temples, Shrines, and Gardens

The spirit of a place is more than the sum of its parts. Indeed, the philosophical question is whether the spirit of a place or of anything else is something *other than* its physical parts. Human beings have contemplated the relationship between spirit and tangible reality since the beginning of recorded language, and likely before that. Various and inconclusive as the answers are, one cannot explore the human landscape of Japan without coming face to face with spirits at every turn (236).

236

Theoreticians of landscape aesthetics who try to explain the spirit of place[16] come up against the fact that the word *spirit* covers what cannot be defined, described, or explained but can only be evoked. I have always liked the statement attributed to Louis Armstrong on jazz music: "If I've got to explain it to you, you'll never understand it." My premise is that the mental activity of *explanation* belongs to one part of our brains and *evocation* to another, and only the older, emotional, mammalian part can evoke the sense of spirit, whatever spirit may be. (Occult tales suggest that dogs see ghosts at least as well as human beings do, and that the minute one tries to reason with a ghost, it vanishes!) Nevertheless, reason is needed to give intelligible form to the intangible spirit of things.

People in preindustrial cultures are generally able to evoke a sense of spirit in their spaces because they take its presence for granted and are not impelled to define it. They do not close off the receptive part of their brains with too much logic. In all cultures, there are talented individuals who manage to implant or evoke the spirit of designed objects and spaces without being able to describe how they do it. The Japanese are remarkable among advanced industrial or postindustrial societies for retaining the primordial sense of place in their otherwise modern world. Perhaps, as I have suggested, this is because they do not feel the need to define spirit in generalized, abstract terms, but concentrate their rational faculties on those aspects of the environment most amenable to logical and measurable ordering. This relates to the creative "innocence" Richie describes, that openness to experience at the root of all artistic (as well as much scientific) activity.

Nowhere is the spirit of place more enchantingly expressed in Japan than in its villas, shrines, and temples set in gardens. These are widely admired and have been written about extensively—I can add little, but I cannot leave this account of Japan without a look at some of those places. For this we had best return to Kyoto. The number of shrines and temples in Kyoto is estimated at between two and three thousand, and the number of private gardens is uncountable.

Kyoto strikes the visitor as a city of green spaces, but it has almost no parks of the Western type; the temple and shrine gardens serve the purpose. The

Buddhist temples maintain a contemplative, restful atmosphere, and the Shinto shrines are often set in sacred spaces one can enter. But in the public areas in front of both there is often a joyous, almost carnival mood: Japanese gods, especially the Shinto *kami*, are part of life, not remote, awesome beings in an astral sphere. Children prance around concession stands as they do in public parks, and the stalls selling religious articles resemble souvenir shops. On a stairway in the Kiyomizudera, there is a man-sized rabbit that made me think of the six-foot rabbit in the Broadway comedy *Harvey* (237). On the street leading to this temple complex, one passes an orange and gold shrine, where people ring

240

gongs on the eaves by pulling long silken ropes to get the attention of the god (238). They clap their hands to send him away as if to say, "Okay, God, I'm done with you now. You can go on about your business." At one shrine in the Kiyomizudera complex, I heard a young woman praying before an avuncular figure of a deity (239). She sounded very much like a child confiding the events of her day to a beloved uncle.

In nearby Nara, the area around the great Todaiji Temple (240)—reported to be the largest wooden structure in the world—is the famous deer park, which the deer sociably share with natives and tourists of all types and ages in a continuous holiday atmosphere. Inside the temple is a giant bronze Buddha, the height of a five-story building, which, despite its immense size, conveys a peculiarly gentle, almost intimate spirit (241). Outside the door, I saw a guide, his hand raised as if he were a small Buddha, expounding on the history of this place to a group of Japanese tourists (242). At the entrance gate to the temple courtyard, visitors are given a benediction by the sacred deer, which freely roam the park (243).

241

242

243

Kyoto's old Imperial Palace, like the palace in Tokyo, is officially a government park, its interior grounds accessible to the public, although one must make a reservation to enter and can do so only in small groups under the direction of a guide and the watchful eyes of rather intimidating guards. My mother gives an amusing account of my father's troubles in getting access to it in 1918, when it was open to none but very important persons.[17] It constituted the residence of the emperors for over a thousand years, from Heian times until the Restoration of 1868, when the Meiji emperor was moved to Tokyo. Indeed, for the two centuries prior to the Meiji period the emperors were virtual prisoners in the Kyoto Palace, while the Tokugawa shoguns ran the country from Edo. The Kyoto Palace is now officially used only for coronations. Yet the palace, behind tile-capped outer walls (244), is maintained at great public expense. Its exquisitely simple wood-framed halls and pavilions stand in fields of raked white gravel (245) on the edge of a magnificent garden (246).

Most of the shrines and temples in Kyoto are accessible to anyone who behaves properly. They are the proxemic epitome of Japanese culture, but they are also distemic places: something at once unique and transcendent in that culture has deep appeal to the human race. Japanese priorities, which have provided the world with Kyoto, are perhaps demonstrated by the famous Golden Pavilion

244

245 246

247

(Kinkakuji) in the northwest corner of the city. Built by one of the Ashikaga shoguns five hundred years ago, it was destroyed by arson in the 1950s and almost immediately rebuilt, complete with real gold leaf, in the midst of the poverty and deprivation of the early postwar years. Today it is open to the view of all who care to visit its tranquil lake and gardens (247). A large portion of trust must accompany the use of all truly distemic spaces. For them to remain distemic, public attitudes must insure that this trust is justified.

A large part of Kyoto is in effect a historic conservation district. I know of no other city in the world as extensively preserved as a cultural monument for the larger society, and in that respect it is a model for all nations. According to Yuga Kariya of the Kyoto City Planning Bureau, the first modern legislative attempt to preserve the city came in 1929 with regulations controlling the height, design, and color of buildings in the surrounding mountains, where there are numerous shrines, temples, and monuments. But it was not until the national Preservation of Historic Landscapes Law of 1966 that Special Conservation Areas were designated, strictly controlling development that would mar the landscape of the hillsides and rivers. But this law did little to protect the character of the central city. Demolition of large historic buildings and small streets of traditional houses to make way

for new buildings caused sufficient public alarm that in 1972 Kyoto established a municipal ordinance on the cityscape.

The 1972 ordinance established Seven Aesthetic Areas surrounding major historic complexes such as the old Imperial Palace and Kiyomizudera. It further designated more than half the urban area as "Restricted Against Enormous Constructions." In addition, it established "Special Preservation Areas for Traditional Buildings," which amounted to the protection of whole neighborhoods. The first of these was along the path to the Kiyomizu Temple at the base of the Higashyama range in the eastern central part of the city. In this area particular attention is given to the protection and maintenance of streets lined with a traditional type of Kyoto townhouse called *kyo-machiya*, which originated in the eighteenth century when Kyoto had a population of 40,000 and was, in Yuga Kariya's words, a "lattice-shaped city."[18] In 1976 the law was amended to provide for the care of whole groups of buildings of this type, with subsidies and architectural advice given to owners who renovate or repair their houses. City policy is not an attempt to preserve the neighborhoods in an unchanging state but a chance to allow residents to renovate in a way that is harmonious with the traditional cityscape. Many of the houses near the major temples have been converted into gift shops and restaurants, but the

248

old scale is maintained (248). Among the districts preserved is the Gion entertainment quarter (132–135).

But official legislation by itself is insufficient to maintain the spirit of a place like Kyoto. There must be widespread public awareness of that spirit and an infinity of small, private actions to foster it, not all of them visible from the street. When I returned to Kyoto in 1984, I tried to locate a man I had known in 1945, the proprietor of an old and distinguished sake brewery, but it was not until another visit a year later that I was able to locate the establishment. It was on a street that seemed familiar, but the old brewery building had been converted into a modern factory, manufacturing medicines under the same family ownership (249). I found that my friend had recently died, but his son and grandson greeted me warmly. Among other things, I asked what had happened to the lovely old house and garden I remembered being above the brewery, and I was told that they were still there. The young man led me to the rear of the building, where, completely out of sight from the street, the unadorned mechanical sheds enclosed an enchanting

traditional Japanese garden. At the end of a serpentine stream with large goldfish, tucked within the warehouse like a pearl in a gray oyster shell, open sliding shoji screens revealed the elegant Meiji-style living room in which I recalled enjoying sake with very good company (250, 251).

249

252

253

254

255

Of the many Kyoto gardens, one of the most
exquisite is that of Byodo-in Temple, south of
Kyoto, which was originally the villa of Prime
Minister Fujiwara-no-Michinaga. His son, who was
the chief advisor to the emperor, converted it into
a Buddhist temple in 1052. The centerpiece is the
Phoenix Hall (252), shaped to resemble the mythical
bird, a most appropriate symbol for Japan.

If I were to select a favorite example of the genius
loci it would be this temple because of its intimate
connection between superbly graceful man-made
constructions and natural objects in time-space (253–
255). The pavilion-with-garden of the Byodo-in
is composed of a seemingly infinite constellation
of living things and inorganic materials, which,
however "natural" in appearance, is wholly contrived
in arrangement, from the grain of a floor plank to
the moss on a stone bridge. Nevertheless, the
contrivance is in accord with the spirit of the
materials, and their interrelationship, their clearly
hierarchical order, evokes a sense of simplicity,
despite their extreme variety and complexity.

256

In photo 256, stepping stones, each formal in its square shape but asymmetrically arranged on the ground, lead by the veranda of a pavilion as if inviting the passerby to wander from side to side while looking around. The clearly articulated railing lies restfully above the cleanly spaced posts. The ends of the rails, turned up at the corners, echo the upturned eaves of the projecting, sheltering roof, which in turn echo the branches of surrounding trees. The stone lantern is placed so as to emphasize the corner of the building and to separate the space one is in from the space beyond. At precisely this point, the meandering stones straighten out purposefully as they lead the pedestrian on into the woods. Thus, the lantern marks a progression in the spatial syntax of this place, separating two subspaces like punctuation between two clauses of a sentence, while integrating them within the whole. Being a manmade structure, the lantern relates to the pavilion, but being free standing it relates to the trees outside.

There are continual surprises in every square foot of space, yet one is left with a profound awareness of the unity of all things and a curious feeling of comprehension and stability. But of course it is all in constant change, as living things are, while its genius loci has presumably remained constant for nearly a thousand years. One author has defined soul as "that which persists through change."[19] In some mysterious way the spirits of the people who build places like this stay with them. Yet the intelligent human energy required to put all the elements of a landscape like Byodo-in together, evoking the spirit of the place and keeping it together through the centuries, is there but not seen. Everything in view is in repose so that even crowds of tourists seem to blend in quietly with the landscape.

In spaces of this sort in Japan, one must marvel at the contradiction that such delicacy, calm, and fundamental gentleness could have been created by fierce lords whose main mission in life was exceedingly bloody and brutal tribal war. It might be argued that the artistry came from the gardenmakers rather than the owners, but that is not true. The shoguns and samurai often took a very personal hand in the design of the buildings and gardens. The Sambo-in garden of the Daigo-ji, not far from Byodo-in, is reported to have been constructed by Generalissimo Hideyoshi himself; he was the second of the powerful rulers who unified Japan before the Tokugawa closed it to the world. In this sense the temple gardens express, as Japan in general does so well, the contradictions of human nature. The long period of peace maintained by the Tokugawa facilitated the development of a high culture, as did the earlier Heian period described in the *Tale of Genji*.

Modern Japanese democracy was built over the old feudal order, which is only a few generations past. Some aspects of this order have survived. In addition to the social hierarchy based on rank and status modern Japanese have inherited a firm ideal of personal discipline from the old samurai class. As a consequence, the discipline required of the fine designer is something to be respected by the public even today, emulated if possible, and always admired. This contrasts strongly with the "six easy lessons" approach in some Western democracies, which assumes that mere self-expression—almost anyone's expression of anything by any means—is art. The samurai warriors not only were expected to master the bloody disciplines of swordsmanship and *seppaku*, but also the disciplined art of poetry. To be a disciplined artist, even if one was not also a warrior, was then and is now a mark of status, a basis for respect, and consequently the public at large seeks as much art as possible in the landscape.

This standard applies to women as well as men, although the position of women in society is by Western standards still very restricted. Chie Nakane notes that a woman in Japan is considered socially unimportant because she lacks status, not because she is a woman, and that a female who manages to achieve public status is in fact highly respected. She herself is a case in point. (It should be noted that the world's first novelist was a Japanese woman, Lady Murasaki, and her thousand-year-old *Tale of Genji* suggests considerable respect for and influence by court women.) When I was a reporter with the Sixth Army in 1945, I interviewed a person my notes say was "Soon Onemura, Japan's most famous woman painter." I was escorted to her home and studio by the cultural editor of the Asahi newspaper, who was also a woman. Onemura, then seventy years old, was introduced by her son, also an artist, who

treated her as if he were attending the emperor. We learned that she had had a long, hard struggle to master the perfection she was after and had now attained it. She sought to portray the purest flower of Japanese womanhood, according to her son's translation, "never vulgar women, no matter how beautiful in face and figure, but only the pure, refined representatives of my sex."

In Haru Matsukata Reischauer's fascinating account of her illustrious grandfather, who began adulthood as a samurai and who became a leader of the Meiji revolution and eventually prime minister, she describes the intense self-discipline he went through in his early training.[20] He was in a sense a self-made man, being adopted rather than born into a samurai family, and despite the discipline, or perhaps because of it, he brought to his career a flexibility of mind and openness to new possibilities characteristic of people who are socially mobile. These types, as I have noted, make up the most distemic portion of the commercial middle class, but I think they also tend to make the finest artists and scientists because they are the most open to new experience. In the life of Matsukata, one can see how, despite all the great changes in outlook and custom that he lived through and helped to bring about, the Japanese reverence for disciplined form continued in his private person and public achievements alike.

The Japanese ability to evoke the spirit of place relates to their view of the world and human society within it as essentially hierarchical. In the egalitarian democracies (as well as the theoretically egalitarian but practically hierarchical Marxist dictatorships), where *equality* is viewed as *sameness*, there is a conceptual delusion. The formula $X = X$ is, for ordinary purposes, not worth the trouble to write out. The formula $X = Y$ is meaningful because it implies that there is something about X that is unlike Y but is equal according to some specific value in a particular context. It is the *differences* between interrelated elements that constitute hierarchy. A hierarchy cannot exist if all elements in a field are the same, and I think that no art can exist without hierarchy. Much as some egalitarians would like to repeal it, hierarchy seems to be a law of the universe, from atoms within molecules and cells within tissues to stars within galaxies. It is part of the realism of the Japanese to recognize this and organize themselves accordingly.

In this regard, the fame of William S. Clark in Japan and his obscurity at home may be instructive. Many of Clark's students at the Sapporo Agricultural College were carefully selected by the Meiji government in Tokyo, and many of them became leaders in the government. They spread his fame. But when Clark returned home, he found himself in trouble with a constituency that had opposed his ambition to teach the children of farmers liberal arts and theoretical science. There were other reasons for his difficulties, some of them financial, but certainly his educational philosophy seems to have been a problem.[21] Americans have traditionally supported public education with enthusiasm, but mainly for the achievement of practical goals for personal advancement by the average citizen.

If one is truly to respect the spirit of a place or of an object designed by human hands, minds, and hearts, one must respect the intense effort of the humans who struggle to give it hierarchical order. To respect the art, one must respect the artist *as artist*. The activities that are universally respected where art is respected have two important aspects, neither of which are likely to be evenly distributed in any population. One is craft, the skill at manipulating physical elements, which takes dedication and concentration and immense amounts of time and effort to learn. The other is talent, a mysterious capacity that is no easier to define than spirit and is somehow related to it (the word "genius" applies to both). In fact, talent can be defined as *the capacity to evoke the spirit in things*. In many professional schools of America and other Western countries, "talent" has become a dirty word, banned as elitist. The word now commonly used to distinguish the work of professional environmental designers is "skills." Statistically, more people can be taught to develop a skill than can be led to develop a talent, and the consequence is that the contemporary public landscape of the Western democracies, where equality is viewed as sameness, has less and less of the genius loci. The answer, of course, is not less democracy but a more realistic— a more natural—concept of democracy.

The German philosopher Hegel formulated the dialectic idea of the unity of opposites, which Karl Marx, in his own words, "turned on its head" by converting it from an idealist concept to a materialist one. In the Hegelian dialectic, opposites are constantly uniting to produce a synthesis of something new, which in turn invokes a new opposite and produces a new synthesis. Marx eliminated from this process the spirit—what remains constant through change—not only standing Hegel's theory on its head, but in effect cutting off the head, or more accurately the heart. Ironically, by eliminating what does not change, he founded what is probably the most inflexible social system ever known. Marx set in concrete the prevailing Western idea that body and spirit are separate and mutually exclusive by eliminating spirit altogether as a matter of social consequence except as it is used as an "opiate" to enslave people.

Whether or not one considers spirit to be something *other than* matter, it can only be made manifest through material form, and this is true whether it preexists in nature or arises only in the human imagination, which, after all, is the product of a physical brain. The heightened awareness of the Japanese to life in the process of constant change leads them to a counterawareness of what persists through change, call it soul or spirit or whatever. I suspect that this is how the Japanese manage to be so spiritual and pragmatic all at once. Throughout this book, I have proposed that this aspect of Japanese culture reflects successfully the natural neural geography of the human brain. It is the sensual, emotional aspect of awareness that responds to change, to the fleeting particularities of moment-to-moment existence. However, it requires abstract thought to see continuity among these sensations of events. In Hegelian terms, then, spirit might be thought of as the synthesis at a given point in space of those united opposites, *sensation* and abstract *idea*.

Traditional Japanese gardens like Byodo-in are perhaps the purest expression of this dialectic, of the linking through art of essentially timeless, spaceless abstract thought with the ephemeral, sensual realities of existence. Japanese abstract thought concentrates on symbolism, in which the *qualities* of one thing are transmuted to another. The materials of garden art are changing plants as well as enduring stones, and the structures are most often made of wood, the most perishable of building materials.

257

Because change is the reality, there is endless variety. A pagoda, for example, is unlike an Egyptian pyramid designed to endure forever. The Egyptian pyramids contained the mummified bodies of the earthly pharaohs in a futile attempt to preserve their living features for all time. One pyramid looks pretty much like another, while every pagoda is different. (I have not seen the pyramids of Egypt, but notwithstanding their similarity in form I have no doubt that they have their own powerful sense of place.) Some Japanese pagodas have five stories, like the one at Tokyo's Asakusa, some three stories, but always an asymmetrical, odd number, never two or four. The posts that support the treelike branching roofs are not continuous and stiff, but jointed so that they can move, and this characteristic flexibility gives them a different sort of permanence in a land of earthquakes and typhoons. A pagoda may be free standing or part of a complex of other structures (257). Although no single pagoda is identical to another, each expresses the constant concept *pagoda*.

Katsura Imperial Villa in Kyoto, now part of the imperial household, emphasizes changing nature somewhat more than enduring human structure. It was started in the early seventeenth century by a Prince Toshihito (who was never a warrior) and completed by his son. A guidebook to this famous place conveys something of the spirit of the owner-architect:

Prince Toshihito had been endowed with a distinguished genius for poetry since his tenderest years. The prince's devotion to the study of classical literature of Japan and China, especially to "Tale of Genji" and the works of Pe Letien, a famous Chinese poet, seems to have influenced him in the design of this villa. The prince liked to paint and play the Koto, a Japanese harp; he learned Ikenobo style of flower arrangement, and also had an opinion of his own about tea ceremony. He did not favor stiffened formalities, and made much of companionship with people.

258

259   260

261

The prince's reported sociability suggests that hierarchy and democracy may not be incompatible. The spirit of Katsura's spaces does seem tolerant and informal compared with Hideyoshi's Byodo-in, but the genius loci, although different, is strong— some might think stronger than that of Byodo-in since Katsura is better known. The Katsura grounds are separated by a bamboo fence from a main road where it crosses the Katsura River. The finely detailed bamboo fence is designed to suggest rusticity and naturalness, which is the main quality of this place. The vertical pickets are echoed by small stakes opposite it on the public way, creating an asymmetrical space between them (258), and there is serene variety within unity in the structure of the fence and in the gate itself (259, 260). The fence is clearly a barrier to unauthorized entry, but the basketlike texture is more protective than exclusionary compared with many of the immense varieties of Japanese fence designs (261). Both attention to detail and reverence for nature in Katsura are shown by the support given an elderly tree beside this fence, under which the river is free to enter unrestricted (262).

262

263

264

Jusuck Koh, addressing the question, Why is Katsura so beautiful? says: "Katsura, as an example of Japanese creativity in garden and architecture, can be considered comparable to the Ryoan-ji stone garden or the Ise Shrines. Katsura, however, is neither for the gods nor for the ascetic life of Zen monks. It is a place for the life of taste, a life possessed neither by materialism and power, nor by the vitality of ordinary culture, yet possessing them all."[22]

Koh suggests, quoting Kenzo Tange, that this place is an expression of the dialectical synthesis between the aboriginal mass culture represented by Shintoism and the aristocratic culture of Zen Buddhism, which was imported from India, China, and Korea. (One could look upon Shinto as the main proxemic force in Japanese culture, and Buddhism as the primary distemic force.) The villa structures of Katsura are in the Shoin style often considered the progenitor of modernism in its rectangular modularity, suggestive of the architecture of Richard Neutra and also, as Koh observes, of the paintings of Mondrian. Scattered throughout the garden on islands and peninsulas around a lake are five tea huts in the Sukiya style, for which the aristocrats adopted the elements of peasant pole buildings with thatched roofs in their search for truth through simplicity and contact with natural materials. The rusticity of

Katsura is indeed restful, but it is an environment highly managed through an understanding of nature in the process of modifying it rather than leaving it to its own devices as in a wilderness. Yet there is more effort here than in Byodo-in to make the composition of buildings and garden appear artless (263, 264).

In the garden of Kyoto's Ryoan-ji Temple, to which Koh compares Katsura, there is actually little vegetation, nothing but a bit of moss here and there. The entire space within a low wall, over which foliage can be seen, is devoted to a number of carefully placed stones in a field of raked gravel, symbolizing many things, depending on whom you talk to, but most commonly the mountains and the sea. The effect is one of truly magical repose. The space is very small, a superb example of a courtyard garden designed to look larger than it is. I knew of this, but was not prepared for how small it really is when I first saw it; all photographs—usually taken with a wide angle lens because one cannot get back from it for a broad view—make it look larger than the real thing. It is meant only to be seen from a platform on one side, not to be entered, a place for contemplation, not action, yet it is very popular with tourists. The genius loci here is unlike anything else in the world (265). The interior spaces of the Kiyomizu Temple on the other side of Kyoto have

266

267

268

269

an equally powerful effect, but by very different means. There, the external space of the platform overlooking central Kyoto (266) is a separate but integral part of the inside space (267), united by the boundary formed by the ritual hand-washing station in which one symbolically cleanses the spirit before entering (268).

Notwithstanding the legendary groupiness of the Japanese, many do like to be solitary when they can find a place for it, and the temples and gardens are designed, among other things, to facilitate this desire (269). Structures in these gardens are placed for contemplation, and they fit the landscape the way fruit fits a tree (270). There is endless variety in the plant materials that are used for these spaces. In one of the Rokko Mountain parks above Kobe, a peaceful space is formed entirely by a forest of bamboo (271).

270

271

272

273   274

275

In the area near the Yashima Plateau north of Takamatsu on Shikoku Island, one finds a roofed gateway to a garden that defines a space without closing it off (272) and a covered bridge that both links and encloses two spaces (273, 274). In this area, also, one comes upon a masonry temple that seems to grow out of the earth. Three precisely positioned and incredibly delicate streams of water flow from scuppers on the roof beams into a still pool (275). Not far away is a shrine featuring the kind of liquid that comes in a bottle and the embodiment of a spirit that expresses the earthy joyfulness of Shinto worship (276).

276

In Takamatsu's Ritsurin Park, built around one
of the finest of the stroll gardens, which was begun
about three hundred and fifty years ago and was
one hundred years in the making, major nodes are
the viewing stations. From them one can pause to
contemplate this garden's complex and intricate
wholeness, always only partially revealed (277). The
attention to detail, which is as characteristic of the
uses of space in places like Ritsurin as it is of
their designs, is perhaps best exemplified by the
ubiquitous stepping stones. To cross a stream on
raised stones one must watch where one is putting
one's feet (278), in the process of which one sees
the stones, the water below them with its currents
and floating leaves and fish, the pebbles underneath
the water, and shimmering reflections of the sky,
foliage on the banks, and even one's own body
(279). The movement of the water is heard if it is
moving. The stones themselves are noticed for their
irregular shapes. They are rarely laid out in a straight
line, and the change of direction, sometimes in
midstream, sometimes where the crossing stones
meet the continuous path of the shore, causes one
to see different views of whatever is ahead. These
are usually a continuous series of surprises, a tea
house appearing among the trees (280), or maybe
an iris garden (281).

279

280

281

282

The tea houses are themselves endlessly varied. In one, the stream one has crossed runs right through the middle of the building, uniting structure and land, so that one is a point on a continuum (282). In another, the guest and the tea cups are the center of a landscape partially visible but wholly present within the open shoji screens (283). The tea cups are laid just so on the mats, but not in a straight line. On the veranda outside, the tea cups are carefully placed in preparation for service or after being used (284). They are part of the design. In Japan everything is part of the design, even—or perhaps especially—the humans who use the space. Any Westerner who has not had long experience in Japan is bound to feel quite literally like a bull in a china shop trying to fit into the pattern.

283

284

A torii gate, sometimes built of dark wood, sometimes bright red, sometimes of stone, will often mark a threshold in the landscape, but again it does not line up symmetrically with the path; instead, it frames another carefully placed object or set of objects, or perhaps has a single stone asymmetrically balanced on one projecting beam. Could the stone on the beam at the upper right of photo 285 be a prank of some passerby? I have been told it is set there for good luck. Whatever it is for, it fits there. The magic of these spaces is that the accidents of change continually become part of the design. This is the only satisfactory way to create a public environment, as no designer ever has full control over everything in the space. But whether the primary change agents are people or nature or both, spirit is evoked in the space if both the artist and the public are attuned to it. In a fountain in a rural park, a stream of water is tuned to fall precisely at a point in a rustic stone basin (286).

287

288

289

In some spaces in Japan, however, time seems to stand still. The gardens have a timeless quality, but the amount of living plant material continually reasserts the present. Man-made structures and artifacts from a previous time, which so effectively engrave the outlook of people long dead on the here and now, perhaps contribute more than natural forms to the sense that the clock has stopped, that

time has stood still in a particular place. I had that
feeling when I visited the town of Kamakura, south
of Tokyo, and Yokohama on Sagami Bay, in the
company of a young Japanese friend for whom its
spaces had strong meanings. For a relatively brief
period in the thirteenth and early in the fourteenth
centuries, Kamakura had been one of Japan's four
capitals, after Nara and Kyoto but before Edo-
Tokyo. Now it is a fashionably historic town, like
Nantucket Island off Cape Cod, where artists and
literati like to live. Here, a whole townscape of
temples and gardens seems preserved (287–290).
Actually, most or all of these structures and spaces
are restored, because the town was dreadfully
battered by the 1923 earthquake that leveled Tokyo
and Yokohama. Haru Reischauer describes her
grandfather Matsukata being pinned under a beam
there when he was in his late eighties and surviving.
She herself was there at the age of eight in a nearby
cottage, and twenty years later she lived out part
of the war in Kamakura.[23] But the restorations give
the feeling that they had always been there.

290

291

292

293

Of all the places I have visited in Japan, the one that is the most haunting for its timelessness in the midst of the changing present is the Itsukushima Shrine on Miyajima Island on the Inland Sea near Hiroshima. This shrine was constructed by a noble named Taira-no-Kiyomori in the twelfth century for the goddess Ichikishima-hime to bring prosperity to his clan. Visitors to the island by boat are greeted by a graceful red torii standing in the water (291). On the hill above it in the village rises a five-storied pagoda (292). A gateway to the village, on the esplanade leading from the boat landing, has a tower lantern that echoes the roof of the torii—both resonate visually with the mountains behind as they have for generations. The gateway also acknowledges the present with a large convex mirror enabling the visitor to see approaching auto traffic from the hillside to the left (293). Moving along the esplanade, visitors are greeted by a statue of some animistic god (294). The gentle harbor is framed by pine trees and stone lanterns—one senses that the goddess of this shrine is very much a citizen of the sea, but also of the towering, mist-shrouded mountains (295). A deer finds something dropped by passing tourists on the stone pattern of the esplanade. Stalls selling souvenirs accentuate rather than conflict with the spirit of this place. We climb a long set of steps up the hill on which the town is perched, and the way, as usual, is indirect (296). The five-storied pagoda rises on the seaward side above the roofs of one of the several shrine buildings (297).

294

295

296

297

298

299

Down below, the brilliant red Marodo Shrine sits on piles above the tidal flats, facing the red torii standing knee deep in the blue harbor (298, 299). At high tide the buildings seem to be floating on the sea. Inside the Maroda Shrine is a stage, the starting point of many festivals and rituals of Itsukushima (300). Nearby is another shrine building dedicated to the ninth-century scholar Michizane Sugawara, who is worshiped as the "deity of learning." A ceremony for composing linked verses was held there every month until the Meiji era.

300

Over it all hovers the spirit of the pines, the mountains, and the sea (301), expansive, eternal, and inclusive. This spirit is the progeny of the particular physical elements of this singular place and the proxemic traditions that have arisen from them, and this spirit will be fully known only to those who have lived their lives here. But it also enfolds into itself—as did the god my mother followed to the river with that joyous crowd in Kyoto—any citizen of the community of strangers who is willing to greet it on its own terms. I believe this capacity of human beings offers the main hope that the quarrelsome, territorial tribes of the human species will be able to collaborate sufficiently to continue to inhabit the numinous spaces of this planet.

301

Notes

Chapter 1. Introduction

1 Edward S. Morse, *Japanese Homes and Their Surroundings* (Rutland, Vt.: Charles E. Tuttle, 1972).
2 Marjorie Barstow Greenbie, *In the Eyes of the East* (New York: Dodd, Mead, 1921), p. xxii.
3 Barrie B. Greenbie, *Spaces: Dimensions of the Human Landscape* (New Haven: Yale University Press, 1981).
4 C. P. Snow, *Two Cultures* (Cambridge: Cambridge University Press, 1959).
5 During the war I kept a journal contained in letters home, totaling hundreds of handwritten pages covering the period from November 1943 to December 1945. Recently I edited these for publication. The quotation is from the edited version dated 25 September 1945.
6 Sydney Greenbie, *Japan, Real and Imaginary* (New York: Harper and Brothers, 1920), p. 286.
7 Ibid., p. 287.
8 Peter Hall, *World Cities* (New York: McGraw-Hill, 1966), chap. 8.
9 Alexis de Tocqueville, *Democracy in America*, ed. Richard D. Heffner (New York: New American Library, 1956).
10 Francine du Plessix Gray, *World Without End* (New York: Playboy Paperbacks, 1981), p. 133.
11 For a fascinating and provocative discussion of this subject, see Jane Jacobs, *Cities and the Wealth of Nations* (New York: Random House, 1984).

Chapter 2. Home Space

1 Morse, *Japanese Homes and Their Surroundings*, p. 241.
2 Teiji Itoh, *Space and Illusion in the Japanese Garden* (New York: Weatherhill, 1965).
3 Ibid., pp. 80–85.
4 Yoshinobu Ashihara, *The Aesthetic Townscape*, translated by Lynne E. Riggs (Cambridge, Mass.: MIT Press, 1983), p. 17.

5 Botond Bognar, *Contemporary Japanese Architecture* (New York: Van Nostrand Reinhold, 1985), p. 60.

6 Lady Murasaki, *The Tale of Genji*, translated by Arthur Waley (Boston: Houghton Mifflin, 1928). A more recent translation was made by Edward G. Seidensticker (New York: Knopf, 1978).

7 Naoki Kurokawa, "Images and Ideas in the Landscape of Japan," Lecture at the University of Massachusetts, Department of Landscape Architecture and Regional Planning, 29 Sept. 1983.

8 Nakane, *Japanese Society*, p. 4.

9 "Japan, A Nation in Search of Itself," *Time*, 1 Aug. 1983, p. 19.

10 Jon Woronoff, *Japan: The Coming Social Crisis* (Tokyo: Lotus Press, 1980).

11 Greenbie, *Spaces*, chap. 2.

12 Alice Coleman, *Utopia on Trial: Vision and Reality in Planned Housing* (London: Hilary Shipman, 1985).

13 Oscar Newman, *Defensible Space* (New York: Macmillan, 1972).

14 Jane Jacobs, *Death and Life of Great American Cities* (New York: Random House, 1961).

Chapter 3. In the Eye of the Beholder

1 Robert Ardrey, *The Territorial Imperative* (New York: Atheneum, 1966).

2 I received a grant from the U.S. National Endowment for the Arts for these travels. The results of the inquiry are summarized in Greenbie, *Design for Diversity* (Amsterdam: Elsevier, 1976).

3 Betty Edwards, *Drawing on the Right Side of the Brain* (Los Angeles: J. P. Tarcher, 1979).

4 Samuel T. Orton, *Reading, Writing, and Speech Problems in Children* (New York: Norton, 1973).

5 Paul MacLean, "The Brain's Generation Gap: Some Human Implications," *Zygon/Journal of Religion and Science* 8, no. 2 (1973): 113–27. MacLean actually finds three basic layers, the innermost of which he calls the "reptilian brain," similar in construction in all vertebrates. This is the area where he finds territorial propensities to be mediated, not the intermediate limbic system found only in mammals. But for my purposes here, two layers, the outer layer involving rational thought processes and the inner layer governing emotional responses to the environment, is sufficiently complex. MacLean has discussed various aspects of his studies in a large number of scientific papers, some of which are listed in the bibliography. A most readable summary for the layperson is Anne H. Rosenthal, *The Archaeology of Effect* (Bethesda, Md.: National Institute of Mental Health, DHEW publication, n.d.). For a more extended discussion of MacLean's theory applied to spatial design and a more detailed bibliography see Greenbie, *Spaces* and *Design for Diversity*.

6 Tadanobu Tsunoda, *The Japanese Brain: Uniqueness and Universality*, translated by Yoshinori Oiwa (Tokyo: Taishukan, 1885). Tsunoda's book was described "doubtful" and "somewhat jingoistic" by a reader of my manuscript who drew it to my attention. However, I myself find nothing whatsoever jingoistic in it, and while I am not competent to judge its scientific validity, it is clearly written (expertly translated) and makes perfect sense to me. Indeed, I found it very exciting.

7 Some years ago, when I was first exploring this subject, I had a number of stimulating conversations with the late John Flynn, who was engaged in brain research at Yale Medical School. He expressed immense admiration for MacLean and his work but did not agree with all of his conclusions. In particular, he did not think that the various parts of the brain referred to functioned as separately as MacLean believes they do. However, if I understand MacLean correctly, he does not claim that they are totally separate, but merely that they can be out of phase with each other and often compete for control.

8 I have suggested that one of the profound ways we differ from other animals is that the symbolic body markings that govern much animal social behavior are expressed by humans in clothing and, even more permanently, are extended away from our bodies into the environment in the form of architecture and other artifacts. See Greenbie, "The Landscape of Social Symbols," *Landscape Research* 7, no. 3 (Winter 1982): 2–6.

9 Donald R. Griffin, *The Question of Animal Awareness* (New York: Rockefeller University Press, 1981).

10 Jane Goodall, *The Chimpanzees of Gombe* (Cambridge, Mass.: Harvard University Press, Belknap Press, 1986).

11 Edward T. Hall, *The Dance of Life: The Other Dimension of Time* (New York: Doubleday, 1983).

12 P. D. MacLean, "The Brain's Generation Gap," *Zygon*, p. 124. The time aspect of MacLean's theory was suggested to me by A. H. Esser, who first drew my attention to MacLean's work. See the record of his pioneering symposium on the use of space by animals and man in A. H. Esser, ed., *Behavior and Environment* (New York: Plenum, 1971).

13 Hall, *The Dance of Life*, pp. 88–89.

14 Stephen and Rachel Kaplan, eds., *Humanscape: Environments for People* (North Scituate, Mass.: Duxbury, 1978), p. 86.

15 Chie Nakane, *Japanese Society* (New York: Penguin, 1970).

16 Isozaki's work is shown in Mildred Friedman, ed., *Tokyo: Form and Spirit* (New York: Harry N. Abrams, 1986), p. 172.

17 Nakane, *Japanese Society*, p. 4.

18 Jean-Claude Courdy, *The Japanese: Everyday Life in the Empire of the Rising Sun*, translated by Raymond Rosenthal (New York: Harper and Row, 1984), p. 262.

19 Ruth Benedict, *The Chrysanthemum and the Sword* (Rutland, Vt.: Charles E. Tuttle, 1954), pp. 41–42.

20 Mitsuru Yoshida, *Requiem for Battleship Yamato*, translated by Richard Minear (Seattle: University of Washington Press, 1985), p. 40.

21 Carl Sagan, *The Dragons of Eden* (New York: Random House, 1977).

22 Robert Hughes, "The Art of All They Do," *Time*, 1 Aug. 1983, p. 48.

Chapter 4. Urban Public Space

1 Donald Richie, *The Inland Sea* (New York: Weatherhill, 1971), p. 290.

2 Courdy, *The Japanese*, pp. 15–16.

3 E. H. Erikson, *Dimensions of a New Identity: The 1974 Jefferson Lectures in the Humanities* (New York: W. W. Norton, 1974).

4 Edward T. Hall, *The Hidden Dimension* (New York: Doubleday, 1966).

5 Greenbie, *Spaces*, chap. 4; see also Greenbie, "Urban Design and the Community of Strangers," *Landscape Design* (June 1984).

6 Yukio Mishima, *The Sound of Waves* (New York: Knopf, 1956).

7 Legibility was found to be the most important element of urban design in the classic study of three American cities by Kevin Lynch, *The Image of the City* (Cambridge, Mass.: MIT Press, 1960).

8 Herbert J. Gans, *The Urban Villagers* (New York: Macmillan, 1962).

9 William H. Coaldrake, "Order and Anarchy: Tokyo from 1868 to the Present," in Mildred Friedman, ed., *Tokyo: Form and Spirit* (New York: Harry N. Abrams, 1986), p. 71.

10 Yuichiro Kojiro, "Edo: The City on the Plain," in Friedman, *Tokyo: Form and Spirit*, p. 44.

11 Geographer R. W. Wilkie, in a most interesting twenty-year study of migration patterns by social class in Argentina, has demonstrated the dynamic nature of the "middle class" as compared to the conservatism of those above and below it, even in a society that would normally be considered "lower class." See Richard W. Wilkie and Jane R. Wilkie, "Environmental Perception and Migration Behavior: A Case Study in Rural Argentina," *International Migration Systems in the Developing World*, ed. Robert N. Thomas and John M. Hunter (Cambridge: Shenckman, 1980), pp. 135–51. See also Greenbie, *Design for Diversity*, pp. 141–43.

12 Kojiro, "Edo: The City on the Plain," in Friedman, *Tokyo: Form and Spirit*, pp. 37–53.

13 Donald Richie, "Walking in Tokyo," in Friedman, *Tokyo: Form and Spirit*, p. 92.

14 Hughes, "The Art of All They Do," p. 48.

15 Frank Lloyd Wright, "In the Cause of Architecture," *Western Architect* (Apr. 1923): 44. Quoted by Kojiro in Friedman, *Tokyo: Form and Spirit*, p. 68.

16 Lynch, *Image of the City*.

17 Jacobs, *Death and Life of Great American Cities*.

18 Edward G. Seidensticker, *Low City, High City: Tokyo from Edo to the Earthquake* (New York: Knopf, 1983).

19 Ibid.

20 Ando Hiroshige, *One Hundred Famous Views of Edo*, introduction by Henry D. Smith II and Amy Porter (New York: George Brazilier, 1986).

21 Seidensticker, *Low City, High City*.

22 Richie, in Friedman, *Tokyo: Form and Spirit*, p. 91.

23 Seidensticker, *Low City, High City*.

24 Richie, *Inland Sea*, p. 203.

25 Seidensticker, *Low City, High City*, p. 137.

26 Ibid., p. 138.

27 Richie, *Inland Sea*, p. 257.

28 Jay McInerney, *Ransom* (New York: Vintage Books, 1985), p. 19.

29 Ibid., p. 227.

30 S. Greenbie, *Japan, Real and Imaginary*, p. 257.

31 Otis Cary, *Mr. Stimson's "Pet City": The Spring of Kyoto, 1945*, Moonlight Series no. 3 (Kyoto: Doshisha University, 1975).

32 Ibid.

33 Ibid.

34 M. B. Greenbie, *In the Eyes of the East*, pp. 180–82.

35 *The City of Kobe*, 1985, p. 13.

36 Ibid., p. 14.

37 Clark's obscurity at home may be ending. As part of an emerging sister-state relationship between Hokkaido and the Commonwealth of Massachusetts, a building containing international programs at the University of Massachusetts in Amherst has been named the William S. Clark House, and a substantial memorial to Clark is being planned at the entrance to the campus.

38 John M. Maki, *Clark: His Glory and Collapse (Kuraaku: Sono Eiko to Zasetsu)*, translated into Japanese by Shinichi Takaku (Sapporo: University of Hokkaido Press, 1978). The irony of Clark's low status as a prophet in his own country is underscored by the fact that the original English manuscript for this book, which sheds an interesting light on nineteenth-century America as well as Meiji Japan, remains unpublished.

39 Jacobs, *Death and Life of Great American Cities*.

40 City of Sapporo, *Sapporo Today* (Sapporo: International Relations Office, 1987), p. 5.

41 Lewis Simons, "A High-tech Expo Opens in Japan's 'City for Science,'" *Smithsonian* (Apr. 1985): 160.

42 This is elaborated in Wilkie, "Environmental Perception and Migration."

43 Ian Baruma, "Work as a Form of Beauty," in Friedman, *Tokyo: Form and Spirit*, p. 146.

44 Some people familiar with Japanese mythology have suggested that the ending of this story refers to the sun *goddess*, not a god, and that the prince's name should be Susa-no-o, legendary brother of Amaterasu, the sun goddess, who wrecked her rice fields and drove her into a dark cave, thereby obliterating the sun from the world, until she was lured out by other gods of

heaven and earth who hung a mirror and a jewel on a tree and performed erotic dances in front of the cave. See Bradley Smith, *Japan: A History in Art* (Garden City, N.Y.: Doubleday, 1964), pp. 138–40. However, I have quoted the story as it was printed on the program of the celebration I attended.

Chapter 5. Green Space

1 Geoffrey and Susan Jellicoe, *The Landscape of Man* (New York: Viking, 1975).

2 Yi-Fu Tuan, *Topophilia: A Study of Environmental Perception, Attitudes, and Values* (Englewood Cliffs, N.J.: Prentice-Hall, 1974).

3 Albert Fein, ed., *Landscape into Cityscape: Frederick Law Olmsted's Plans for a Greater New York City* (Ithaca: Cornell University Press, 1967).

4 Makoto Nakamura, "The Twofold Beauties of the Japanese Garden," *Proceedings of the 23d World Congress of the International Federation of Landscape Architects, Japan 1985*, pp. 260–63.

5 Sadatoshi Tabata, ed., "Landscape Architecture in Japan from 1964 to 1985," *Journal of the Japanese Institute of Landscape Architects* 48, no. 4 (1985): 54.

6 Akira Sato and S. Shimoyama, *Landscape Planning and Recreation in Japan* (Tokyo: Parks and Open Space Association of Japan, 1985).

7 Michael R. Reich, "Environmental Policy and Japanese Society," *International Journal of Environmental Studies* 20 (1983): 191–207.

8 Seidensticker, *Low City, High City*, pp. 116–18.

9 Haru Matsukata Reischauer, *Samurai and Silk: A Japanese and American Heritage* (Cambridge, Mass.: Harvard University Press, Belknap Press, 1986), pp. 290–98.

10 Seidensticker, *Low City, High City*, pp. 70–73, 123.

11 Kiichiro Nakai, Susumu Ishida, and Kimio Kondoh, "Park Planning Based on Conservation of the Natural Environment in the Mountains and Hills of Kobe—Proposals for the 'Forest of Kobe,'" *Proceedings, 1985*, pp. 96–101.

12 Bognar, *Contemporary Japanese Architecture*, p. 88.

13 Richie, *Inland Sea*, p. 64.

14 Yoshida, *Requiem for Battleship Yamato*.

15 Richie, *Inland Sea*.

16 Vincent Scully, *The Earth, the Temple, and the Gods* (New Haven: Yale University Press, 1962). See also Christian Norberg-Schultz, *Genius Loci: The Phenomenology of Architecture* (New York: Rizzoli, 1980).

17 M. B. Greenbie, *In the Eyes of the East*, pp. 197–99.

18 Yuga Kariya, "Conservation of Landscape and Cityscape in Kyoto" (Kyoto: Planning Bureau, Kyoto City Government), p. 4.

19 Quoted from William Barrett, *Death of the Soul*, by Jenny Teichman, *New York Times Book Review*, 7 Sept. 1986, p. 24.

20 Reischauer, *Samurai and Silk*.

21 Maki, *Clark*.

22 Jusuck Koh, "Katsura: Why Is It So Beautiful?" *Landscape Architecture* 74, no. 5 (Sept.–Oct. 1984): 116.

23 Reischauer, *Samurai and Silk*, p. 150.

Bibliography

Ardrey, Robert. *The Territorial Imperative*. New York: Atheneum, 1966.

Ashihara, Yoshinobu. *The Aesthetic Townscape*. Translated by Lynne E. Riggs. Cambridge, Mass.: MIT Press, 1983.

Bergue, Augustin. "Some Traits of Japanese Fudosei." *Japan Foundation Newsletter* 14, no. 5 (Feb. 1987): pp. 1–8.

Bognar, Botond. *Contemporary Japanese Architecture*. New York: Van Nostrand Reinhold, 1985.

Benedict, Ruth. *The Chrysanthemum and the Sword*. Rutland, Vt.: Charles E. Tuttle, 1954.

Cary, Otis. *Mr. Stimson's "Pet City": The Sparing of Kyoto, 1945*. Moonlight Series no. 3. Kyoto: Doshisha University, 1975.

Courdy, Jean-Claude. *The Japanese: Everyday Life in the Empire of the Rising Sun*. Translated by Raymond Rosenthal. New York: Harper and Row, 1984.

Coleman, Alice. *Utopia on Trial: Vision and Reality in Planned Housing*. London: Hilary Shipman, 1985.

Dazai, Osamu. *Return to Tsugaru: Travels of a Purple Tramp*. Tokyo: Kodansha, 1985.

Edwards, Betty. *Drawing on the Right Side of the Brain*. Los Angeles: J. P. Tarcher, 1979.

Erikson, E. H. *Dimensions of a New Identity: The 1974 Jefferson Lectures in the Humanities*. New York: W. W. Norton, 1974.

Esser, A. H. *Behavior and Environment*. New York: Plenum, 1971.

Friedman, Mildred, ed. *Tokyo: Form and Spirit*. New York: Harry N. Abrams, 1986.

Fromm, Erich, D. T. Susuki, et al. *Zen Buddhism and Psychoanalysis*. New York: Harper and Brothers, Colophon, 1970.

Gans, Herbert J. *The Urban Villagers*. New York: Macmillan, 1962.

Goodall, Jane. *The Chimpanzees of Gombe*. Cambridge,

Mass.: Harvard University Press, Belknap Press, 1986.

Greenbie, Barrie B. *Spaces: Dimensions of the Human Landscape*. New Haven: Yale University Press, 1981.

———. *Design for Diversity*. Amsterdam: Elsevier, 1976.

———. "Urban Design and the Community of Strangers." *Landscape Design* (June 1984).

Greenbie, Majorie Barstow. *In the Eyes of the East*. New York: Dodd, Mead, 1921.

Greenbie, Sydney. *Japan, Real and Imaginary*. New York: Harper and Brothers, 1920.

Gray, Francine du Plessix. *World Without End*. New York: Playboy Paperbacks, 1981.

Griffin, Donald R. *The Question of Animal Awareness*. New York: Rockefeller University Press, 1981.

Edward T. Hall. *The Dance of Life: The Other Dimension of Time*. New York: Doubleday, 1983.

———. *The Hidden Dimension*. New York: Doubleday, 1966.

Hall, Peter. *World Cities*. New York: McGraw-Hill, 1966.

Higuchi, Tadahiko. *The Visual and Spatial Structure of Landscapes*. Translated by Charles Terry. Cambridge, Mass.: MIT Press, 1983.

Hughes, Robert. "The Art of All They Do." *Time*, 1 Aug. 1983, pp. 45–48.

Hoban, Phoebe. "The Brain Race." *Omni*, June 1985, pp. 73–124.

Inoue, Mitsuo. *Space in Japanese Architecture*. Translated by Hiroshi Watanabe. New York: Weatherhill, 1985.

Itoh, Teiji. *Space and Illusion in the Japanese Garden*. New York: Weatherhill, 1965.

Jacobs, Jane. *Cities and the Wealth of Nations*. New York: Random House, 1984.

———. *Death and Life of Great American Cities*. New York: Random House, 1961.

"Japan, A Nation in Search of Itself." *Time*, 1 Aug. 1983.

Jellicoe, Geoffrey and Susan. *The Landscape of Man*. New York: Viking, 1975.

Jung, Carl G. *The Spirit in Man, Art, and Literature*. Translated by R. F. C. Hull. Princeton: Princeton University Press, 1966.

Kaplan, Stephen and Rachel, eds. *Humanscape: Environments for People*. North Scituate, Mass.: Duxbury, 1978.

Koestler, Arthur. *The Ghost in the Machine*. London: Hutchinson, 1967.

Koh, Jusuck. "Katsura: Why Is It So Beautiful?" *Landscape Architecture* 74, no. 5 (Sept.–Oct. 1984): 115–25.

Komatsu, Sakyo. *Japan Sinks*. Translated by Michael Gallagher. New York: Harper and Row, 1976.

Lynch, Kevin. *The Image of the City*. Cambridge, Mass.: MIT Press, 1960.

McInerney, Jay. *Ransom*. New York: Vintage Books, 1985.

MacLean, Paul. "The Brain's Generation Gap: Some Human Implications." *Zygon/Journal of Religion and Science* 8, no. 2 (1973): 113–27.

———. "The Brain in Relation to Empathy and Medical Education." *Journal of Nervous and Mental Disease* 144 (1967): 374–82.

———. "Contrasting Functions of Limbic and Neocortical Systems of the Brain and Their Relevance to Psychophysiological Aspects of Medicine." *American Journal of Medicine* 25, no. 4 (1958): 611–26.

———. "Special Award Lecture: New Findigs on Brain Function and Sociosexual Behavior." In *Contemporary Sexual Behavior: Critical Issues in the 1970s*, edited by Joseph Zubin and John Money. Baltimore: Johns Hopkins University Press, 1973.

MacLean, Paul, T. J. Boag, and D. Campbell. *A Triune Concept of the Brain and Behavior*. Toronto: University of Toronto Press, 1973.

Maki, John. *Kuraaku: Sono Eiko to Zasetsu (Clark: His Glory and Collapse)*. Translated into Japanese by Shinichi Takaku. Sapporo: Hokkaido University Press, 1978. The original English manuscript, *William Smith Clark: A Yankee in Hokkaido*, is available in the University of Massachusetts archives.

———. *We the Japanese*. New York: Praeger, 1972.

Maquet, Jacques. *The Aesthetic Experience: An Anthropologist Looks at the Visual Arts*. New Haven: Yale University Press, 1986.

Minear, Richard H. "Cross-Cultural Perception and World War II." *International Studies Quarterly* 24, no. 4 (Dec. 1980): 555–80.

Mishima, Yujio. *The Sound of Waves*. New York: Knopf, 1956.

Morse, Edward S. *Japanese Homes and Their Surroundings*. Rutland, Vt.: Charles E. Tuttle, 1972.

Murasaki, Lady. *The Tale of Genji*. Translated by Arthur Waley. Boston: Houghton Mifflin, 1928. More recently translated by Edward G. Seidensticker. New York: Knopf, 1978.

Nakane, Chie. *Japanese Society*. New York: Penguin, 1970.

Newman, Oscar. *Defensible Space*. New York: Macmillan, 1972.

Norberg-Schultz, Christian. *Genius Loci: The Phenomenology of Architecture*. New York: Rizzoli, 1980.

Persig, Robert M. *Zen and the Art of Motorcycle Maintenance*. New York: Bantam, 1974.

Reich, Michael R. "Environmental Policy and Japanese Society." *International Journal of Environmental Studies* 20 (1983): 191–207.

Reischauer, Edwin O. *The Japanese*. Cambridge, Mass.: Harvard University Press, Belknap Press, 1977.

Reischauer, Haru Matsukata. *Samurai and Silk*. Cambridge, Mass.: Harvard University Press, Belknap Press, 1986.

Richie, Donald. *The Inland Sea*. New York: Weatherhill, 1971.

Rudofsky, Bernard. *The Kimono Mind*. London: Victor Gollancz, 1966.

Sagan, Carl. *The Dragons of Eden*. New York: Random House, 1977.

Sanford, Anthony J. *The Mind of Man: Models of Human Understanding*. New Haven: Yale University Press, 1987.

Sato, Akira, and S. Shimoyama. *Landscape Planning and Recreation in Japan*. Tokyo: Parks and Open Space Association of Japan, 1985.

Scott, A. C. *The Flower and the Willow World*. London: William Heinemann, 1959.

———. *The Kabuki Theatre of Japan*. New York: Macmillan, 1966.

Seidensticker, Edward. *Low City, High City: Tokyo from Edo to the Earthquake*. New York: Knopf, 1983.

Shogun Age Exhibition Executive Committee. *Shogun: The Shogun Age Exhibition*. Nagoya, Japan: Tokugawa Art Museum, 1983.

Simons, Lewis. "A High-tech Expo Opens in Japan's 'City for Science.'" *Smithsonian* (Apr. 1985): 159–64.

Smith, Bradley. *Japan: A History in Art*. Garden City, N.Y.: Doubleday, 1964.

Smith, Richard Allen. "Comfort, Room Use, and Economy of Means in the Japanese House." *Building and Environment* 16, no. 3 (1981): 167–75.

Snow, C. P. *Two Cultures*. Cambridge: Cambridge University Press, 1959.

Suzuki, D. T. *Zen and Japanese Buddhism*. Tokyo: Japan Travel Bureau, 1970.

Tabata, Sadatoshi, ed. "Landscape Architecture in Japan from 1964 to 1985." *Journal of the Japanese Institute of Landscape Architects* 48, no. 4 (1985).

de Tocqueville, Alexis. *Democracy in America*. Edited by Richard D. Heffner. New York: New American Library, 1956.

Tsunoda, Tadanobu. *The Japanese Brain: Uniqueness and Universality*. Translated by Yoshinori Oiwa. Tokyo: Taishukan, 1885.

Van der Post, Laurens. *Yet Being Someone Other*. New York: William Morrow, 1982.

White, James W. *Migration in Metropolitan Japan: Social Change and Political Behavior*. Berkeley: University of California Institute of East Asian Studies, 1982.

Woronoff, Jon. *Japan: The Coming Social Crisis*. Tokyo: Lotus Press, 1980.

Yi-Fu Tuan. *Topophilia: A Study of Environmental Perception, Attitudes, and Values*. Englewood Cliffs, N.J.: Prentice-Hall, 1974.

Yoshida, Mitsuru. *Requiem for Battleship Yamato*. Translated by Richard Minear. Seattle: University of Washington Press, 1985.

List of Places Illustrated

Subject and Photograph Index

Note: Page numbers are in roman; photograph numbers are in italic.

racial diversity, 42; superiority, 42

railroads, 4, 63, 130; stations, 7, 9, 31, 63, 64, 65, 71, 74, 87, 91, 108; *166*

rationality, 40, 41, 43, 48, 52, 70, 91, 94, 97, 140

reality, 11, 45, 46, 47, 49, 70, 151; manifested by art, 69; "real Japan," 56; "real you," 12, 46

reason: gives form to spirit, 140; with a ghost, 140

recreation, 113, 116, 117, 127, 134

reforestation, 116

Reischauer, Edwin O., 52

Reischauer, Haru Matsukata, 108, 151, 167

religion, 46, 84, 97, 104, 105

research, basic, 94

residential districts, 119

respect for artist, 151

restaurants, 24

rice, 136; agriculture, 105; farmers, subsidies to, 135; terraces, 136; *224–27, 230*

Richie, Donald, 52, 55, 57, 63, 68, 69, 70, 71, 82, 133, 139, 140

Ritsurin Park, 133, 162; *277–81*

rituals, 54, 56, 71, 159; handwashing before temple, *268*; Kagura, 101, *156–59*; Neputa, 98, *153–55*

rivers, 84, 172; dead, 121; Kamo, 73; Katsura, 73; parks, 114, 126, *207–10*; in hotel lobby, 87; Toyohira, 91; Yodo, 73

robotics, 96

Rokko Island, 88; mountain range, 116; parks, 159

Roman Empire, 62

romantic landscape, 104, 105

roofs, 139, 150, 157

Roppongi, 4, 66; *1*

Rousseau, Jean-Jacques, 104

rudeness, 54

Rural Toy Museum, Kurashiki, 140; rusticity, 157

Ryoan-ji Temple, 157; *265*

sacred deer, 143, *243*

sacred garden, Heian shrine, 82, *126–28*

sacred spaces, 141

safety, 53, 94

Sagami Bay, 167

Sagan, Carl, 49

Saint Augustine, 139

Saint George, 101

Saitama Memorial Park, 106

sake, 101, 146, 161; *276*

Sakutiki, 116

Sambo-in garden of the Daigo-ji, 150

samurai, 55, 66, 68, 98, 150, 151

Sanjusangendo, 81

Sapporo, 89–94, 117, 128, *144–49, 211, 212;* Agricultural College, 93; Botanical Gardens, 117, 125; Citizen's Charter, 93; Clock Tower, 93; Sculpture Garden, 119; *189–91*

Savannah, 139

scale, 7, 33, 40, 53; mammalian, 47

science, 3, 11, 42, 46, 47, 48, 52, 53, 85, 90, 104, 140, 152; scientists, 40, 95, 151

Science City, 96–97

sculpture, 87, 119; snow, 100; urban park, 110

security, 27, 40, 52; in the familiar, 96

Seidensticker, Edward, 52, 66, 69, 108, 112; Seidensticker Syndrome, 52

self-expression, 151

sensuality, 43–45, 47–49, 53, 60, 69, 152; of car designs, 46

separation of body from spirit, 104

Seto Inland Sea, 116; *216–21*

Seto-naiki National Park, 133

shakkei, 17

Shibuya, 64; *89–91*

Shikoku, 133, 161

Shinjuku, 59, 61, 63, 65, 96, 114; *81, 92–95, 181*

Shinkansen (bullet train), 9, 62, 130; *10*

Shinobazu Pond, 110; *174*

Shinto, 27, 45, 47, 83, 84; grove, 83, 84, 157, 161, *126–27*; music and dance, 101, 105; as proxemic and Buddhism as distemic, 157; shrines, 141; City, 96

Shitamachi, 66

shoes, removing, 20, 23, 24

shoguns, 55, 68, 132, 150

Shoin style, 157

shoji screens, 9, 14, 16, 146, 164; *16, 19, 24, 34*

shopping centers, 92, 93, 112

shrines, 81, 104, 105, 110, 132, 140, 141, 168; *115, 125–28, 160, 238, 239, 275, 276, 291, 298–301*

Shukkeien Garden, 124; *201–03*

similarities, 11, 54

Simons, Lewis, 95

sin, 70

Singapore, 45

single family houses, 31, 34

situation, 44, 46, 48, 54, 97

Sixth Army, 151

skills, 97, 152

skyscrapers, 4, 61; *82, 181*

Snow Festival, 100

social: agencies, 47; biology, 42, 45; characteristics, 55; conduct, 48; conscience, 91; context, 97; corridor, 91; danger, 28; distance, 53; hierarchy, 151; ideas, Rousseau's, 104; landscape, dimensions of, 54; life, Edo, 68; pattern, 54; precedence, 46; relationships, 47; science, 40; socially mobile people, flexibility of, 151; spatial network, 33; status 12, 31, 52, 55; territory, 43, 54, 56

society, 11, 12, 27, 28, 40, 52, 54; group-oriented, 97; traditional 43, 46, 47; individual emphasizes attribute, 97; postindustrial, 140; rural, 55

sociologists, 70

sordidness, 69

soul, 152; that which persists through change, 150

souvenirs, 141, 168

veranda, 16, 33, 150, 164; *17, 21, 124*

view, 24; from floor, 23; of the Inland Sea, 133, *219–20;* passion for, 133

viewing stations, 162; *219*

village, 40, 53, 55, 104, 168; as frame, 46; historic, 128, out-of-the-way, 139

villas, 140, 157

visitors, 52, 56, 70, 89, 107; national parks, 134

wa, 20, 27, 43, 47

Wakayama, 3

walls, 14, 20, 24, 31, 33, 40, 52, 54, 70, 71, 104, 157; around units of human thought, 97; of hills, 77; of mountains, 86

war: cold, 52; memorial, Hiroshima, 120; nuclear, 96, 120; with China, 106; tribal, 150. *See also* World War II

Warner, Langdon, 81

West, 3, 4, 7, 9, 11, 12, 45–60 passim, 69, 92, 97, 98, 151

Western, 55; concepts, 90; chauvinism, 94; facial features, 67; cities, 64; culture, 43, 45, 46; democracies, 152; park style, 116; Westerners, 14, 38, 44, 46, 104, 164

Wheeler, William, 93

Whitney, Clara, 69, 83

wilderness, 104, 157; parks, 106

women, status of, 151

woodlands, 106

work ethic, 63

workplace, 27, 47, 54

World War II, 2, 7, 27, 48–73 passim, 84, 86, 97, 105, 106, 112, 121, 123, 133

Wright, Frank Lloyd, 60, 61; *84*

xenophobia, 52

Yamanote, 66

Yasaka Shrine, 77, 81; *115*

Yashima Plateau, 161

Yi-Fu Tuan, 11

yin-yang, 24

Yodo River, 73, 126; *207–10*

Yokohama, 31, 167

Yoshida, Mitsuru, 48, 133

Yoshiwara, 68

Yoyogi Park, 114; *182*

Zen Buddhism, 157

zoning, 34

zoological garden, Ueno Park, 110